Secrets of JERUSALEM'S Temple Mount

Secrets of JERUSALEM'S Temple Mount

LEEN AND KATHLEEN RITMEYER

Illustrations by Leen Ritmeyer

with foreword by Hershel Shanks,
editor of *Biblical Archaeology Review*

Biblical Archaeology Society
Washington, DC

Designed by Sean Kennedy

Editorial and production staff: Angela Botzer, Gabrielle DeFord,
Steven Feldman, Lauren Krause, Christen Long, Lisa Josephson Straus,
Judy Wohlberg, Bridget Young

Ritmeyer, Leen, 1945-
Secrets of Jerusalem's Temple Mount/Leen and Kathleen Ritmeyer;
with foreword by Hershel Shanks.
p.   cm.
Includes biographical references.
ISBN 1-880317-52-4

1. Temple of Jerusalem (Jerusalem) 2. Temple Mount (Jerusalem)
3. Jerusalem—Antiquities. 4. Excavations (Archaeology)—Jerusalem.

I. Ritmeyer, Kathleen, 1952- .   II. Title
DS109.3.R57   1998
933—dc21   98-27110
CIP

© 1998
Biblical Archaeology Society
4710 41st Street, NW
Washington, DC 20016

Reprinted from *Biblical Archaeology Review*
November/December 1989
March/April 1992
January/February 1996

Cover image by Richard Nowitz

CONTENTS

FOREWORD

Few archaeological sites hold the fascination of the Temple Mount in Jerusalem. Here was the site of Solomon's magnificent Temple, the House of the Lord. Here the exiles returned from Babylonia and built their modest Second Temple. And here Herod, called the Great, rebuilt the Second Temple as one of the wonders of the world. Here Jesus walked and turned over the tables of the money changers.

Does this entirely explain the extraordinary fascination of the site? Not quite. Perhaps it is the tension between how little is known and how much could be known. The evidence is there. But the site has not even been surveyed—looked at—for more than a century and a quarter, and excavations, even small probes, are forbidden. The site is now graced by one of the most breathtaking buildings from the ancient world to have survived wholly intact—the Dome of the Rock, built in the eighth century A.D. by the city's Arab rulers. The Crusaders turned it into a church when they conquered Jerusalem, but now, once again, Muslims control the Dome of the Rock, as well as the huge platform on which it sits, which they call Haram el-Sharif (the Noble Sanctuary) and much of the world calls the Temple Mount.

So we are largely dependent on history books, Englishman Charles Warren's survey in the 1860s, and visible clues on and around the Temple Mount for an understanding of the site that holds so much of our common past.

Yet, surprisingly, there is much to be learned despite these limitations. Through the careful detective work of Leen Ritmeyer, an intrepid Dutchman who lived in Jerusalem for 16 years (and in Israel a total of 22 years), we can piece those clues together into an essentially new picture.

Ritmeyer is an architect who, in 1973, succeeded Brian Lalor as the architect attached to the mammoth archaeological excavation south of the Temple Mount, begun in 1967, after the Six-Day War, by Professor Benjamin Mazar of Hebrew University. Ritmeyer continued as architect to the expedition until 1978, when the excavation ended.

In 1989 Ritmeyer left for England to pursue a doctorate in archaeology at the University of Manchester, earning his Ph.D. in 1992. He is now revising his dissertation in light of recent discoveries he has made. The subject: the Temple Mount, of course. By now he is the world's leading expert on the archaeology of the Temple Mount.

Ritmeyer is ultimately interested in the Temple itself. But his method was to first understand the Temple Mount, in the hope that this would lead him to better understand where the Temple was located. This, in turn, has enabled him to identify the very spot where the Ark of the Covenant rested. I should immediately add that there is no certainty in these things, but I do believe that he has come as close as anyone has to solving these problems. And he doesn't simply make assertions; he gives you his reasoning so you can reach your own conclusion, based on the evidence. I, for one, think he makes quite a good case.

But, in a way, that's beside the point. Much of the excitement lies in the journey. You will learn so much along the way, regardless of the decision reached at the end of the line. The development of the Temple Mount is, in itself, a fascinating story. Ritmeyer also provides a comprehensive description of the excavations all around the Temple Mount, painting a vivid picture of life in Jerusalem at the time of Jesus and Herod the Great. You will even learn about the geography of Jerusalem. And all this is supplemented by Kathleen Ritmeyer's lovely description of a walk through Jerusalem at the turn of the era.

Once the Temple Mount has been reconstructed, it is possible to consider from an entirely new viewpoint where the Temple was located. Ritmeyer delves into the century-old records of Sir Charles Warren, who carefully examined and meticulously recorded all the nooks and crannies, the cisterns and tunnels, the holes and dead ends of the Temple Mount. With Warren's records and his understanding of the Temple Mount's development, Ritmeyer is able to identify the site of the Temple.

Finally, he takes the last step—locating the exact spot where the Ark of the Covenant rested. Time and again, he will surprise you with the evidence he is able to identify. It is there—why hadn't anyone noticed it before?

The journey you are about to take is an exciting one. It is also demanding. But it will well repay the effort. Learn and enjoy. And be inspired.

Hershel Shanks
Editor, *Biblical Archaeology Review*

1

RECONSTRUCTING HEROD'S TEMPLE MOUNT IN JERUSALEM

Leen and Kathleen Ritmeyer

Herod the Great—master builder! Despite his crimes and excesses, no one can doubt his prowess as a builder. One of his most imposing achievements was in Jerusalem. To feed his passion for grandeur, to immortalize his name and to attempt to win the loyalty of his sometimes restive Jewish subjects, Herod rebuilt the Temple (indicated by a 1 on the drawing on pp. 12-13) in lavish fashion. But first he extended the existing platform—the Temple Mount—on which it was built, doubling its size.

Herod ruled from 37 to 4 B.C. Scarcely a generation after the completion of this unparalleled building project,[1] the Romans ploughed the Temple Mount and built a temple to Jupiter on the site. Not a trace of Herod's Temple was left. The mighty retaining walls of the Temple Mount, however, were deliberately left lying in ruins throughout the Roman (70-324 A.D.) and Byzantine (324-640) periods—testimony to the destruction of the Jewish state. The Islamic period (640-1099) brought further eradication of Herod's architecture. Although the Omayyad caliphs

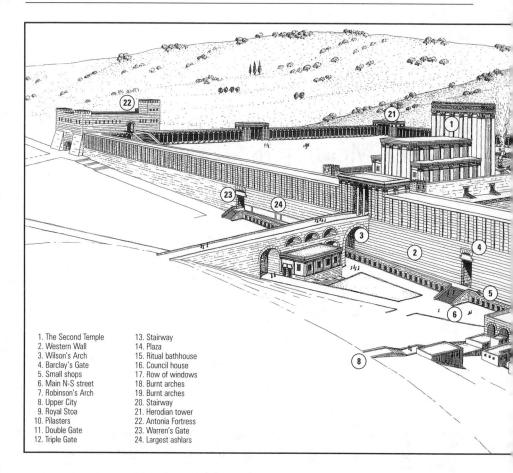

1. The Second Temple
2. Western Wall
3. Wilson's Arch
4. Barclay's Gate
5. Small shops
6. Main N-S street
7. Robinson's Arch
8. Upper City
9. Royal Stoa
10. Pilasters
11. Double Gate
12. Triple Gate
13. Stairway
14. Plaza
15. Ritual bathhouse
16. Council house
17. Row of windows
18. Burnt arches
19. Burnt arches
20. Stairway
21. Herodian tower
22. Antonia Fortress
23. Warren's Gate
24. Largest ashlars

THE TEMPLE MOUNT. When King Herod (37-4 B.C.) rebuilt the Temple (1), he carried out the project on a grandiose scale. Not satisfied with the size of the Temple Mount that Solomon had built, Herod doubled its extent by lengthening the eastern wall, in the background, at each end and by building a new wall on the other three sides. To this he added the monumental stoa (9) along the southern wall, right foreground, a series of gates—some with simple stairways, others adorned with magnificent stairways—and a bridge (3), at left, linking the mount with the Upper City (8). The Antonia Fortress (22), at the far left, was built to guard the Temple Mount's vulnerable northern side, the only side lacking a natural valley that could give protection to the mount.

This glimpse at grandeur is the product of painstaking excavations, insightful interpretations and the skilled hand of architect-artist Leen Ritmeyer, who translates the evidence into a vision of the past. Using photos, drawings and words, Ritmeyer and his wife Kathleen conduct the reader on a tour around the wall surrounding the Temple Mount. They employ archaeological and literary evidence to reconstruct the ancient appearance and function of all the major features of the wall and its gateways during the Herodian period. The reconstruction seen here, with the western wall extending to the left and the southern wall extending to the right, can serve as a visual guide to this chapter. Features discussed in the text, and the photos and plans that illustrate them, are keyed by numbers to their locations in this drawing.

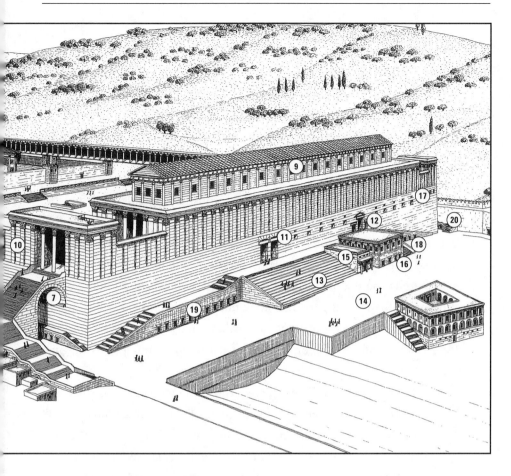

(whose dynasty lasted from 633 to 750 A.D.) repaired a large breach in the southern wall of the Temple Mount, the entire area of the mount and its immediate surroundings was covered by an extensive new religio-political complex, built in part from Herodian ashlars that the Romans had toppled. Still later, the Crusaders (1099-1291) erected a city wall in the south that required blocking up the southern gates to the Temple Mount. Under Ottoman rule (1517-1918), Jewish prayer at the Western Wall was again permitted, but the Turkish sultans changed the entire character of the Temple Mount by Islamicizing it, so as to make it virtually unrecognizable.

With nothing to go on but literary sources (principally the writings of the first-century A.D. Jewish historian, Josephus) and the bare outline of the retaining wall, it is no wonder that the imaginations of artists over the centuries reigned supreme as they sought to reconstruct the Temple Mount and its immediate environs.

A realistic reconstruction of the area around the Temple Mount became possible only when systematic excavation of the area south and west of it began in 1968, soon after the 1967 Six-Day War. Directed by Professor Benjamin Mazar, on behalf of the Israel Exploration Society and the Hebrew University of Jerusalem, the excavation continued without a break until 1978.

Also of considerable assistance in reconstructing this area are the records of the British explorer Sir Charles Warren, who investigated the Temple Mount environs during the 1860s on behalf of the London-based Palestine Exploration Fund. Warren and his companions dug numerous shafts down to bedrock, as well as horizontal underground tunnels off the shafts to trace long-buried walls and other structures. During the Mazar excavations, we rediscovered some of Warren's tunnels, which amply demonstrated the daring and courage his digging methods required.

As Professor Mazar's dig progressed, each wall and stone was surveyed, each architectural element examined. Gradually a complete plan of the multiperiod site—from the eighth century B.C. in the Iron Age to the Turkish period—emerged. To reconstruct what the area was like in the time of Herod the Great, the Herodian elements were separated from the other periods. Then we re-examined the ancient sources and searched for parallels in other monumental Hellenistic buildings in an effort to arrive at an accurate reconstruction. A series of architects assisted the archaeologists, of whom Leen Ritmeyer, one of the authors of this article, was the latest.[2]

Of the Temple itself, we shall not speak.* The Muslim authorities, under whose jurisdiction the Temple Mount lies, do not permit archaeological investigation of the platform. Suffice it to quote Josephus's observation, "To approaching strangers [the Temple] appeared from a distance like a snow-clad mountain; for all that was not overlaid with

---

*For a detailed description of Herod's Temple, according to Josephus and Mishnah *Middot* (a rabbinic source), see Joseph Patrich, "Reconstructing the Magnificent Temple Herod Built," *Bible Review*, October 1988.

gold was of purest white" (L., *The Jewish War* 5.5.6).*

Our reconstruction concentrates on the walls of the Temple Mount, the means of access to the Temple Mount, the gates in the walls and the adjoining streets and buildings. In short, we will make a circuit around the Temple Mount and trace the remains that tell the tale of Herod's greatness.

Let us begin at the Western Wall (2).** It was this fragment of masonry that became the focus for the longing of dispersed Jews throughout the centuries. Then it was known as the Wailing Wall; now it is called the Western Wall or simply *ha-Kotel*, the Wall. Today it is again a center of worship, and also a site of national celebration. Contrary to common understanding, this wall is not a remnant of the Solomonic Temple Mount.

In order to build his Temple to the Israelite God, Yahweh, Solomon needed to construct a level platform on the highest hill of Jerusalem. To accomplish this, Solomon built a retaining wall to support the earthen fill of the platform, the Temple Mount. Herod doubled the area of this platform by building a new wall on three sides—west, south and north—and by extending the fourth wall (the eastern wall) north and south to meet the new southern and northern walls. Today's Western Wall is a section of the massive retaining wall Herod built to support the Temple Mount.

In enlarging the Temple Mount, Herod not only doubled the original area of the Temple podium, he also wrought a complete change in the topography of the area. The Tyropoeon Valley, which bordered the Temple Mount on the west, was filled in, as was a small valley to the north of the old Temple Mount. In the south, the upper slope of the Kidron Valley was filled in, leaving only the line of the eastern wall unchanged.

Josephus described Herod's retaining wall as "the most prodigious work that was ever heard of by man" (W., *Antiquities of the Jews* 15.11.3).

An idea of the size of Herod's Temple Mount can be conveyed by stating that it would take approximately five football fields to fill its area from

---

*The quotations from Josephus's works come from the Loeb Classical Library edition (abbreviated "L.," comprising *The Jewish War*, tr. H. St. J. Thackeray, and *Jewish Antiquities*, tr. Ralph Marcus and Allen Wikgren) or from *The Works of Josephus*, tr. William Whiston (abbreviated "W.").

**Numbers in parentheses in this chapter correspond to numbered features in the drawing on pp. 12-13.

Plan of the Temple Mount Wall

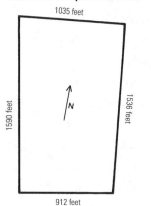

1035 feet

1590 feet

1536 feet

912 feet

N

north to south and six football fields from west to east. Its exact dimensions are shown in the drawing, at left; note that it is not exactly rectangular.

At the present time, only seven courses of Herodian ashlars are visible above the prayer plaza in front of the Western Wall. Below the plaza level are 19 additional courses of Herodian ashlars. This means that bedrock lies a staggering 68 feet below the plaza. (The shafts dug by Warren adjacent to the Wall show us how many courses lie below the surface. These shafts can still be seen north of the prayer area. They are well lit; coins thrown by tourists reflect from the bottom.)

It is not difficult to distinguish Herodian ashlars from those of later periods above them. Herodian masonry has a fine finish, a flat, slightly raised center, called a boss, and typical flat margins around the edges. The stones were cut with such precision that no mortar was needed to fit them together perfectly. Some of these ashlars are as much as 35 feet long and weigh up to 70 tons.

North of the open prayer area, under overhead construction, is Wilson's Arch (3), named after Charles Wilson, the British engineer who first discovered it in the mid-19th century. As it exists today it is probably not Herodian, but a later restoration, the first of a series of arches built to support a bridge that spanned the Tyropoeon Valley, linking the Temple Mount with the Upper City to the west. In Herodian times an aqueduct also ran over this causeway, bringing water from "Solomon's Pools" (not really Solomonic) near Bethlehem to the huge cisterns that lay beneath the Temple platform.

Moving south from Wilson's Arch, we come to a gate in the Western Wall. Known today as Barclay's Gate (4)—after its discoverer, J. T. Barclay, a British architect who worked in Jerusalem a short time before Wilson and Warren—it has been almost completely preserved. The only section now visible, however, is the northern half of its massive lintel (almost 27 feet long and 7 feet high) and the top three stones of its northern doorpost. These form part of the Western Wall at the southern end of the area today reserved for women (by Orthodox Jewish law, men and women

WILSON'S ARCH. *Discovered by the British engineer-excavator Charles Wilson in the mid-19th century, Wilson's Arch (3) supported a bridge and aqueduct that spanned the Tyropoeon Valley to connect the Temple Mount with the Upper City. Today's arch is apparently a later restoration rather than the original Herodian structure. Originally the arch rose some 74 feet above the bedrock of the Tyropoeon Valley, but partial filling of the valley has reduced the arch's height to 25 feet above the present pavement. The arch is 45 feet wide. Today the reconstructed arch shelters an area where Jews pray and where Torah scrolls—often carried outdoors to be read*

in the plaza before the Western Wall—are stored. The first-century A.D. Jewish historian, Josephus, mentions the Hasmonean forerunner of this bridge in connection with the Roman siege of Jerusalem by Pompey in 63 B.C. The Hasmonean forces retreated into the Temple area and "cut the bridge."

worship separately). The remainder of the gate is obscured by the earthen ramp leading up to the Moor's Gate, which is the present-day access to the Temple Mount from this area.

We know the level of the original threshold of Barclay's Gate from Warren's records. Our excavation revealed the level of the Herodian street in front of the gate. There is a difference of about 13 feet between the level of the street and the level of the threshold of Barclay's Gate. This difference rather baffled us until another bit of seemingly trivial information, recorded by the indefatigable Warren, provided the missing piece of the puzzle.

Warren tells us that while digging in the area, he saw the remains of a vaulted chamber protruding from below the threshold of Barclay's Gate. Warren assumed that this must have been part of a lower viaduct that crossed the Tyropoeon Valley, but on a much smaller scale than the bridge supported by Wilson's Arch. Additional clues from our excavation

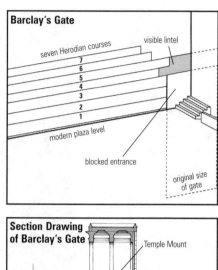

Barclay's Gate

seven Herodian courses

7
6
5
4
3
2
1

modern plaza level

visible lintel

blocked entrance

original size of gate

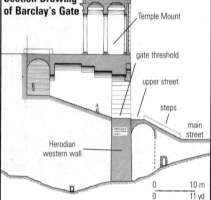

Section Drawing of Barclay's Gate

Temple Mount

gate threshold

upper street

steps

main street

Herodian western wall

0   10 m
0   11 yd

BARCLAY'S GATE. *Although most of Barclay's Gate (4) survives, little of it can be seen today. Named for its discoverer, the 19th-century British architect J. T. Barclay, this gate in the Western Wall of the Temple Mount has mostly disappeared behind later construction and beneath the risen street level. The sketch (top right) indicates the original Herodian elements visible in the larger photo, as well as the unseen parts of the gate. Seven courses of Herodian ashlars are visible in the Western Wall. The first three courses above plaza level formed the upper part of the gate's northern doorpost. Small stones now block half of the upper part of the gate's former doorway. The other half of the blocked doorway is obscured by the earthen ramp and wall leading up to the Moor's Gate, the current entrance to the Temple Mount. The wall at right in the larger photo, perpendicular to the Temple Mount's Western Wall, supports the ramp. Almost half of Barclay's Gate's massive lintel is visible (outlined in the photo), extending from above the doorpost across the top of the blocked doorway. In its entirety, the lintel measures about 27 feet long and 7 feet high.*

Excavation in front of Barclay's Gate revealed that the Herodian main street (6) (smaller photo) in front of the gate lies 13 feet lower than the gate's original threshold. It had been a mystery how people reached Barclay's Gate from the main street, so far below. But now we have an answer.

The bottom reconstruction drawing shows Barclay's Gate as it would appear if sliced down the middle, and then viewed from the north. A vaulted chamber between the main street and the gate threshold above apparently supported an upper street and a stairway from the main street. This upper street ran along the western wall from the southwest corner (where steps leading up to the upper street were found; see photo, p. 29) to Warren's Gate (23). The space beneath the upper street was probably partitioned into small rooms by walls built perpendicularly to the western wall. Two such walls were excavated. These rooms may have been shops (5), serving the bustling traffic of pilgrims and residents.

have led us to conclude that this vault supported a staircase that led up to Barclay's Gate from the main Herodian street. At the southern corner of the western wall, we found a flight of six steps, 10 feet wide, leading north. Somewhat farther north (about 46 feet south of Barclay's Gate), we found two walls built perpendicular to the western wall. A row of many similar walls, perpendicular to the southern wall, had been found earlier. These we assume to be the remains of commercial premises frequented by visitors to the Temple. If that is true, the two walls perpendicular to the western wall probably also formed part of a similar arrangement of small cells on this side (5). The flight of steps at the southern end of the western wall must therefore have led up to a narrow street that ran *over* the roofs of these shops. Finally, the vault observed by Warren must have carried a staircase that connected the lower street (the main street [6]) with this narrow upper street, giving access to Barclay's Gate. Thus, the 13-foot difference between the level of the main Herodian street and the threshold of Barclay's Gate was now explained.

The fact that the main Herodian street stopped short of the western wall by 10 feet strongly supports this reconstruction. The small shops adjacent to the western and southern walls formed part of the upper and lower markets of the city, as described by Josephus. The main Herodian street ran from Damascus Gate in the north to the Siloam Pool in the south, through the Tyropoeon Valley; the shops adjacent to the western wall of the Temple Mount fronted on this street.

The next element we will examine is Robinson's Arch (7), which protrudes from the western wall south of Barclay's Gate. In fact, Robinson's Arch is barely the spring of the arch, in contrast to Wilson's Arch, which is complete. Robinson's Arch is named after American orientalist Edward Robinson, who in his travels in Palestine in the second third of the 19th century correctly identified dozens and dozens of Biblical sites. It was he who first identified this arch that bears his name. From its discovery until the time of our excavation, it was generally assumed that Robinson's Arch was the first of a series of arches that supported another causeway spanning the Tyropoeon Valley in the same way as the bridge that began at Wilson's Arch. At the beginning of our excavations, a hypothetical reconstruction based on this theory was indeed drawn up. However, when we found no other piers in addition to those that had supported Robinson's Arch, and that had already been discovered by Warren, we turned in perplexity to Josephus. He described the gate to the Temple Mount that must have existed above Robinson's Arch as follows:

> The last gate [in the western wall] led to the *other* city where the *road descended down into the valley* by means of *a great number of steps* and thence up again by the ascent.
>
> W., *Antiquities of the Jews* 15.11.5.

According to Josephus, this gate led from the Temple Mount, not *over* the Tyropoeon Valley via a bridge to the Upper City (8) on the west, but rather to "the valley" below by means of "a great number of steps." Access to the "other city," the Upper City on the west, was obviously via steps leading up from the valley.

Excavations proved the accuracy of Josephus's description. The archaeologists discovered a series of piers of arches of graduated height, ascending from south to north. The arches were equidistant. At the top is a turn eastward over Robinson's Arch. On this basis a monumental stairway has been reconstructed leading from the Royal Stoa (9) on the Temple Mount down to the street in the Tyropoeon Valley. From there one could ascend to the Upper City or walk south into the Lower City.

Beneath Robinson's Arch, weights, coins, stone vessels and other evidence of commercial activity were found in four small cells. Above the lintel of the entrance to each of these shops was a relieving arch designed to distribute the downward pressure of the superstructure.*

The stairway that ascended over Robinson's

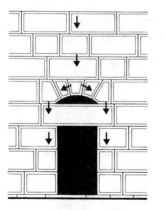

---

*A relieving, or discharging, arch is an arch built into the wall above the lintel of a doorway. Without it, the pressure of the higher courses would break the lintel stone. The relieving arch diverts the pressure to the side parts of the opening, as illustrated in the drawing at left. Arrows show diversion of pressure from above.

Arch provided an impressive entrance to the Royal Stoa which Herod built on the southern end of the Temple Mount. Josephus describes this royal portico in some detail (L., *Jewish Antiquities* 15.11.5). It was built in the shape of a basilica with four rows of 40 columns each. Each of the huge columns in this veritable forest of columns was 50 feet high. The thickness of each was such, Josephus tells us, "that it would take three men with outstretched arms touching one another to envelop it" (L., *Jewish Antiquities* 15.11.5). Fragments of columns found in the excavation validate Josephus's description. Most of these fragments, however, had been reused in later Byzantine and Islamic buildings.

It was probably from this Royal Stoa that Jesus

> drove out all who sold and bought in the Temple, and he overturned the tables of the money changers and the seats of those who sold doves. He said to them, "It is written, 'My house shall be called the house of prayer'; but you make it a den of thieves."
>
> Matthew 21:12-13; Mark 11:15-17; Luke 19:45-46

Lying on the main north-south street adjacent to the western wall, the excavators found massive amounts of rubble, testifying to the extensive destruction of the complex inflicted by the Roman general Titus in 70 A.D. Among the various architectural remains found in the rubble were steps from the original monumental stairway, arch stones, columns, capitals, friezes and pilasters.

These pilasters are of special interest because they confirm the architectural style of the wall of the Temple Mount: flat in the lower part, with pilasters, or engaged pillars (10), in the upper part. These rectangular engaged pillars were set into the wall and topped with capitals.

A complete Herodian wall in this same style has survived intact in the structure surrounding the Tomb of the Patriarchs (Machpelah) in Hebron.*

On the Herodian street near the southwest corner of the Temple

Text continues on page 24

---

*See Nancy Miller, "Patriarchal Burial Site Explored for First Time in 700 Years," **BAR**, May/June 1985; and Dan Bahat, "Does the Holy Sepulchre Church Mark the Burial of Jesus?" **BAR**, May/June 1986.

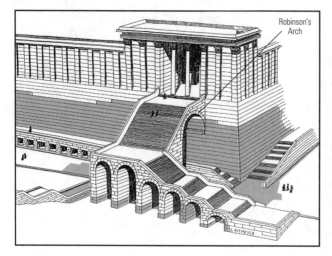

ROBINSON'S ARCH.

Discovered by Edward Robinson (1794-1863), often hailed as the "father of Biblical geography" (top, right), Robinson's Arch (7) was assumed to be the first of several supporting a bridge over the Tyropoeon Valley from the Temple Mount to the Upper City, similar to the bridge that began at Wilson's Arch (3). Before excavation, only a trace of an arch's spring (right) jutting from the deeply buried western wall hinted at the original Herodian structure. Excavation uncovered the full extent of the spring, the protruding stones halfway up the wall at left (opposite), but failed

to find the piers that would have supported a bridge across the valley. Instead, the archaeologists dis-
covered a series of piers of graduated height in a north-south line south of Robinson's Arch. The piers were
supports for the arches of a monumental stairway, which led up from the main street in the valley and
then turned right to the entrance to the Royal Stoa. Robinson's Arch, in this reconstruction (opposite,
upper left), would have supported the upper portion of the stairway, attached to the Temple Mount wall.
Shaded areas in the drawing identify Herodian remains visible today.

Mount, the excavators found a large stone block with a Hebrew inscription carved on it. Unfortunately, the end of the inscription is not on this fragment. The piece containing the final letters of the inscription had broken off, leaving the inscription open to various interpretations. The surviving part of the inscription can be vocalized *l'bet hatqia l'hak ...,* which may be translated "to the place of trumpeting *l'hak-* ...."

Various possibilities have been suggested to complete *l'hak—l'ha-kohn* (for the priest); *l'hekal* (toward the Temple); or *l'hakriz* (to herald [the Sabbath]).* Whatever the correct ending, it is clear that this inscription was a direction to the place where the priest stood to blow the trumpet to announce the commencement of the Sabbath and feast days as mentioned in Josephus (*The Jewish War* 4.9.12). Most scholars have assumed that the direction was for the priest himself, to mark the place where he was to stand. Another possibility, however, is suggested by traces of fine white plaster found on parts of the stone. These traces indicate that the inscription itself may not have been visible after the stone was in place. The entire inscription may simply have been a mark inscribed in the quarry to indicate to the builders where to place the stone. The fact that the carving is not particularly beautiful would support this theory.

One thing is clear, however: the stone could have come only from the top of the southwest corner of the Temple Mount. Found lying on the Herodian street, underneath other stones that had fallen from the tower above, it could not have been transported here from any other place. The tower at the southwest corner of the Temple Mount stood at a height of approximately 50 feet above the level of the Temple court. The Romans would never have moved the stone from another part of the Temple precincts and then hoisted it up to the tower and dropped it on the pavement before destroying the tower. The fact that the inscription is incomplete gave rise to theories that the original location of the trumpeting stone was elsewhere.** Here is one instance where Warren's excavation method—the digging of shafts and tunnels—detracted from, instead of

---

*See Aaron Demsky, "When the Priests Trumpeted the Onset of the Sabbath," **BAR**, November/December 1986.

See Asher S. Kaufman, "Where Was the Trumpeting Inscription Located?" letter in **BAR, May/June 1987.

THE ROYAL STOA. The largest structure on the Temple Mount, this grand hall extended across the southern end of the great platform from east to west (see drawing, pp. 30-31). Built in the style of a basilica, the stoa was divided into a central nave and side aisles by four rows of 40 columns each (plan, right).

One row consisted of pilasters built into the southern wall. A second row, 40 monoliths topped by Corinthian capitals, created an aisle adjacent to the nave. A third row divided the nave from an aisle on the other side. The fourth, northernmost row formed an open colonnade, not a wall as on the southern side. Through this open row of columns one could proceed into the Temple court.

At the eastern end of the nave, the apse (drawing below) was the setting for meetings of the Sanhedrin—the supreme Jewish legislative, religious and judicial body. In his proud description of the Temple Mount, Josephus called this stoa "more deserving of mention than any under the sun" (Antiquities of the Jews XV:412).

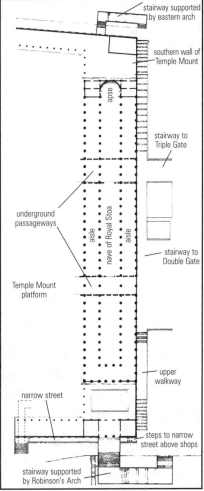

stairway supported by eastern arch

southern wall of Temple Mount

stairway to Triple Gate

stairway to Double Gate

underground passageways

aisle

nave of Royal Stoa

aisle

apse

Temple Mount platform

upper walkway

narrow street

steps to narrow street above shops

stairway supported by Robinson's Arch

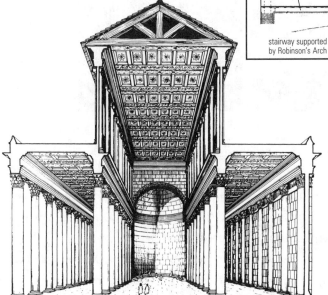

THE KORBAN VESSEL. A fragment of a stone vessel (at right), found in the fill near the southern wall, bears the inscribed word krbn (korban), which means "sacrifice." As seen in this wax impression (below), two crudely drawn birds, identified as pigeons or doves, also appear upside down and below the word on the fragment. The vessel may have been used in connection with a sacrifice to celebrate the birth of a child, since these birds were traditional offerings on such an occasion. The sale of these birds was targeted by Jesus when he "drove out all who sold and bought in the Temple, and he overturned the tables of the money changers and the seats of those who sold doves" (Matthew 21:12; Mark 11:15).

ISRAEL ANTIQUITIES AUTHORITY (IAA)

ERICH LESSING (IAA)

supplemented, our understanding of the remains. Warren almost certainly cut off the remainder of the inscription on this stone while digging his shaft in darkness at the southwest corner of the Temple Mount. Happily, he was unaware of the controversy that would rage when the stone was uncovered some hundred years later.

Let us turn now to the southern wall of the Temple Mount (see drawing, pp. 30-31). Even before our excavations began, the locations of its two main features, the Hulda Gates (named after a prophetess—see

2 Kings 22:14; 2 Chronicles 34:22), were known. The remains of these gates are visible in the wall we see today. They are now referred to as the Double Gate (11) and the Triple Gate (12). Few people are aware,

Text continues on page 30

PILASTERS. Rectangular engaged pillars, or pilasters, decorated the upper portion of the Temple Mount wall (10). An example from another Herodian structure, the enclosure wall of the Tomb of the Patriarchs (Machpelah) in Hebron, appears in the drawing at right. Remains of the Temple Mount pilasters were found in the rubble in front of the pier of Robinson's Arch (below). In this view we stand in front of the Temple Mount's western wall, out of sight at lower left. The large, broken stone in the foreground is a wall fragment with a piece of a protruding pilaster; it lies in front of the nearly buried entrance to one of the shops beneath the upper street. The shop's beautifully dressed lintel is topped by two semicircular stones. Just to the left of the semicircular stone on the left is another pilaster fragment, with fine carved margins. At lower left, three stone steps formerly supported by Robinson's Arch lie where they fell, still in neat order.

DE VOGÜÉ, LE TEMPLE DE JERUSALEM

THE PLACE OF THE TRUMPETING. Many courses of fine Herodian masonry still stand at the southwest corner of the Temple Mount (opposite, top). Beneath the unexcavated bank of earth abutting the Temple Mount's western wall, four steps are exposed—part of a stairway. This stairway once ascended to a narrow street that ran over the rooftops of a row of shops (5) along the Temple Mount's western wall. Another major street (6) ran in front of the shops.

On the smooth paving stones of the Herodian street in front of the steps, at the right of the photo, a wooden frame erected by the excavators protects a large stone that fell there in 70 A.D. The eight-foot-long ashlar bears a dramatic, but incomplete, Hebrew inscription (below), "to the place of trumpeting to [or "for"] ... " Although the excavators who discovered the stone in 1969 made an earnest search for the missing fragment, it was never found. Very likely, 19th-century explorer-archaeologist Charles Warren inadvertently broke the stone. Digging his excavation shaft, seen as a dashed line in the drawing (opposite, bottom), through fill that buried the southwest corner, Warren pierced the Herodian pavement at this corner and probably cracked the edge of the trumpeting stone, which lay where it had fallen on the pavement, one end protruding into his shaft.

inscription

לבית התקיעה לחכ"ד

What does the inscription mean? Scholars have offered several suggestions for the missing words: "to the Temple," "to herald the Sabbath," "for the priest." However the inscription ended, it gives us hard evidence that atop the Temple Mount walls, above the southwest corner shops, there was a designated place for a priest to stand and announce with a trumpet blast the beginning or end of the Sabbath (drawing, opposite). Josephus, the first-century A.D. Jewish historian, in The Jewish War, describes this very spot: "Above the roof of the priests' chambers, ... it was the custom for one of the priests to stand and to give notice, by sound of trumpet, in the afternoon of the approach, and on the following evening of the close, of every seventh day, announcing to the people the respective hours for ceasing work and for resuming their labors."

channel cut to hold Byzantine water pipes

outline of Warren's excavation shaft

inscribed stone broken by Warren's shaft

steps to narrow upper street over shops

however, that the Double Gate has been preserved in its entirety inside the Temple Mount. Its original lintel and relieving arch are still intact. On the outside, the western half and most of the eastern half of the Double Gate are concealed by a Crusader structure built against the southern wall of the Temple Mount in order to protect the Double Gate during the Crusader period. At that time, the southern wall of the Temple Mount served as the city wall, and the center of government itself was located on the Temple platform. The security of the Double Gate required the erection of a massive tower outside it to provide a zigzag entrance. Standing perpendicular to the southern wall of the Temple Mount, the wall that obscures most of the Double Gate on the outside was part of this Crusader tower.

Over the remaining part of the Double Gate still visible on the outside is a decorative applied arch that dates from the Muslim Omayyad period. Originally, however, there was no decoration, or even molding, on the outside.

Inside the Double Gate, which gave access to the Temple court, two pairs of domes still delight the eye with their stone-carved decoration.

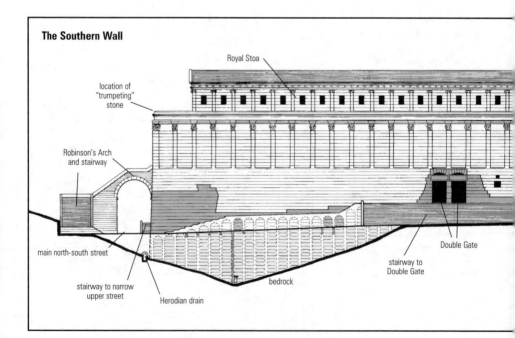

The Southern Wall

Royal Stoa

location of "trumpeting" stone

Robinson's Arch and stairway

main north-south street

stairway to narrow upper street

Herodian drain

bedrock

stairway to Double Gate

Double Gate

Using floral and geometric motifs, these unique decorations are fine examples of how Herodian craftsmen adapted Roman decorative styles while still conforming to Jewish law, which forbade the representation of human or animal figures.

Some earlier reconstructions of the outside of this gate included additional decoration, such as a pediment (a triangular, roof-shaped decoration above the lintel of a doorway) or a frieze. However, by counting each of the Herodian courses and drawing up an accurate elevation of the whole southern wall, we were able to determine that the top of the relieving arch above the lintel of the Double Gate was level with the internal court. So there would have been no room for any additional decoration. Today's courtyard level—2,420 feet above sea level—is the same as the Herodian court level. I (Leen) was able to confirm this in 1977 during repairs to the floor of the El-Aqsa mosque, which lies above the Double Gate. At that time, just below the floor, I saw a circular keystone—the top of the dome of the Double Gate.

In Herodian times, access to the Double Gate from outside was chiefly by means of a broad stairway (13), founded on the natural bedrock of

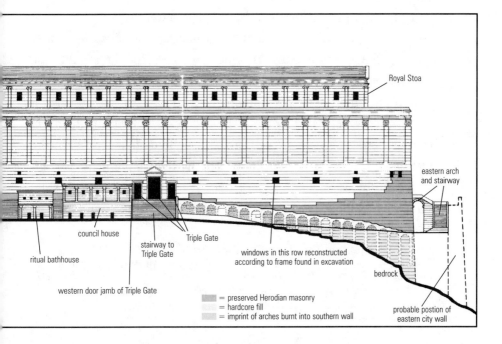

the Temple Mount slope. The stairway's eastern end extends 105 feet east of the centerpost of the Double Gate. In our reconstruction we have assumed that the stairway was built on the central axis of the Double Gate so that it, therefore, also extended 105 feet west of the Double Gate's centerpost. Accordingly, the total width of the stairway is shown to be 210 feet—an impressive entranceway indeed! The 30 steps, which were laid alternately as steps and landings, were conducive to a slow, reverent ascent. This monumental stairway also provides a pictorial setting for an incident described in the Talmud,* in which we are told, "Rabban Gamaliel and the elders were standing at the top of the stairs at the Temple Mount" (Tosefta, *Sanhedrin* 2:2).

From the viewpoint of design and town-planning, it is evident that a wide plaza (14) must have existed south (in front) of the steps leading to the Double Gate. Paving stones in a small area, approximately 16 feet square, that withstood the ravages of time confirm the existence of this plaza. The rest of the paving slabs were taken by later builders who needed construction material. Approximately 100 feet south of the steps, the archaeologists found evidence of what was probably the foundation of the plaza. This suggests that the dimensions of the plaza were what we should expect them to have been. Its size was apparently comparable to similar plazas in the ancient world, at such places as Athens, Priene and Assos.

Between the Double Gate and the Triple Gate, our reconstruction drawing shows two buildings. The one to the west (15) was a bathhouse for ritual purification; many *mikva'ot* (ritual baths) cut into the bedrock have been found there. The building to the east (16) was probably a council house, indicated by the many bedrock-cut Herodian chambers (rooms) found near the Triple Gate. This building may have been the first of the three courts of law located in the Temple precincts, as mentioned in the Mishnah:** "One [court] used to sit at the gate of the Temple Mount, one used to sit at the gate of the Temple court and one

---

*The Talmud (tahl-MOOD) is a collection of Jewish laws and teachings comprising the Mishnah and the Gemara (a commentary an the Mishnah). There are two Talmuds. The Palestinian (or Jerusalem) Talmud was completed in the mid-fifth century A.D.; the Babylonian Talmud, completed in the mid-sixth century A.D., became authoritative.

**The Mishnah is the collection of Jewish oral laws compiled and written down by Rabbi Judah the Prince in about 200 A.D.

used to sit in the Chamber of Hewn Stone" (*Sanhedrin* 11:2).

If the Double Gate was for pilgrims to enter and exit, the Triple Gate was used by members of the priestly order to reach the storerooms where the wine, oil, flour and other items needed in connection with the Temple service were kept. From there, of course, they could also reach the Temple platform.

On either side of the Triple Gate, we have reconstructed a row of windows (17). Their existence has been supposed on the basis of a finding in the immediate area, a window frame with grooves for metal bars. Some provision for light and air was needed for the underground storeroom. This fact, combined with the window frame, is the basis for the windows we have reconstructed.

Excavations found the area near the southeast corner of the Temple Mount to be devoid of architectural remains, as it had served as a quarry for construction during later periods. Our workers cleared away the accumulated rubble from the wall, thereby exposing the original stones. One day, while surveying the bedrock foundations of Herodian rooms that adjoined the southern wall on the outside, east of the Triple Gate, we noticed something unusual. The imprint of arches burnt into the stones was clearly discernible on the Herodian wall. These arches descended in height toward the southeast corner of the Temple Mount. They were all that remained of small cells, probably shops (18), that lay below the stepped street that skirted the Temple Mount wall.

The tragedy of the Roman destruction comes vividly to life as we imagine the only possible scenario that would have left such an indelible imprint on the southern wall. The limestone ashlars used in the Herodian construction can be reduced to powder when exposed to very high temperatures. The Roman soldiers must have put brushwood inside the chambers; the blaze created when this was set alight would have caused the arches to collapse. The street that was carried by these arches also collapsed. Before the arches collapsed, the fire burnt into the back wall of the chambers, leaving the imprint of the arches as evocative testimony to the dreadful inferno. Josephus writes that, after having burnt the Temple, "The Romans, thinking it useless, now that the Temple was on fire, to

Text continues on page 36

THE DOUBLE GATE. *The main entrance to the Temple Mount at the time of Herod is marked today by half of an arch (photos, left) built over the Double Gate during the Omayyad period (633-750 A.D.). Used by pilgrims and residents of Jerusalem, including Jesus, to approach and exit the sacred precinct, the Double Gate originally was not decorated at all on the outside. Instead, it was surmounted by a plain lintel and above this, a relieving arch (drawings below). The Herodian lintel and relieving arch are visible in the photos directly above the applied Omayyad arch. A fragment of another, smaller Omayyad decoration protrudes from the wall above the relieving arch.*

The wall extending perpendicularly from the gate at left in the photos is part of an entrance tower erected by Crusaders. The Crusaders walled up the eastern opening of the 20-foot-high Double Gate and built their entrance tower in a zigzag shape to protect the Double Gate's western opening (plan, opposite, far right). In the fine reconstruction drawn by Count Melchior de Vogüé in 1864 (bottom left) we can see how the arches looked before the Crusader tower blocked them. The tower wall is distinguishable by a rectangular blue tint overlay. The architectural features to the right of the tinted area are those visible in the photos (left). Everything beneath and to the left of the tint is now hidden by the remains of the Crusader tower.

RICHARD NOWITZ

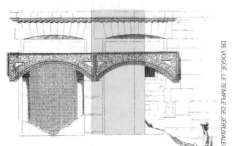

DE VOGÜÉ, LE TEMPLE DE JÉRUSALEM

doorway leading from eastern passageway into chambers below Royal Stoa

All structures tinted dark blue are original Herodian structures

DE VOGÜÉ, *LE TEMPLE DE JERUSALEM*

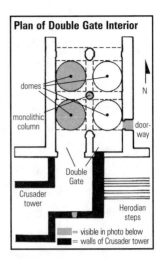

Plan of Double Gate Interior

domes

monolithic column

N

door-way

Double Gate

Crusader tower

Herodian steps

= visible in photo below
= walls of Crusader tower

Thirty steps—*partially original and partially restored—*
led up to the Double Gate. Their heights are roughly equal,
between 7 and 10 inches. However, their depths alternate—12
inches, then 35 inches, then 12 inches, and so on. In this way, the Temple Mount architect created an
ascent that required each worshipper to approach the Temple slowly and with some deliberation. In the
photo (opposite, left top), at the top of the steps, huge Herodian ashlars form the first course of stones
in the southern wall east—to the right—of the Double Gate. The smaller stones above the ashlars date
from rebuilding work in the Omayyad period.

Although the exterior of the Double Gate was modest, within it elaborately carved columns and
domes adorned a passageway to the Temple Court, giving the visitor a preview of the Temple's splen-
dor. As shown in the drawing (opposite, right), the first four domes and the supporting side walls and
columns stand today in their original form; here we see the interior of the gate from the outside; we
are looking north.

In the photo (bottom) we see the two intact western domes from the opposite direction—from within
the passageway, looking south toward a sunlit window in the wall of the Crusader tower. Flowers and
geometric designs cover the dome ceil-
ings. Though stylized, these flowers represent specific local species. In the
northwestern dome, a border of acan-
thus leaves frames a scallop design. In
the southwestern dome a grapevine
twines among eight decorated squares
(drawing, above).

In the lit area on the left of the
photo of the interior, beyond the large
horizontal concrete beam, is the eastern
passageway of the Double Gate. On the
eastern wall of the passageway—at the
far left of the photo—a doorway leads
into side chambers located below the
Royal Stoa. The doorway's extant
Herodian lintel and relieving arch are
visible behind and left of the modern,
concrete frame around a white
Herodian column. In the drawing
(opposite, right) this doorway is at
the right.

GARO NALBANDIAN

spare the surrounding buildings, set them all alight, both the remnants of the porticoes and the gates ..." (L., *The Jewish War* 6.5.2).

In the western part of the southern wall (19), three similar arches were subsequently discovered burnt into the wall. Two flights of three steps each, with a landing in between, still exist near the southwest corner. The continuation of this pattern of steps and landings along the southern wall from west to east reaches exactly to the top of the first visible burnt arch. From the third visible arch (which is, at its center, 282 feet east of the southwest corner), a sharp flight of steps has to be inserted to reach the level of the top of the stairway leading to the Double Gate.

Now let us proceed to the eastern wall of the Temple Mount, which today has a Muslim cemetery in front of it. Some 130 feet of this ancient wall were exposed by a bulldozer prior to 1967. Despite the lack of scientific excavation on this side of the Temple Mount, many clues to its former appearance are preserved in the jigsaw of stones that make up the wall. Three Herodian windows, one with its lintel still in place, can be discerned in the Herodian tower just north of the southeast corner. This tower loomed high above the Kidron Valley and is sometimes identified as the "pinnacle of the Temple" referred to in Jesus' temptation in the wilderness (Matthew 4:5; Luke 4:9).* Some 100 feet north of the corner (directly opposite Robinson's Arch on the western wall) the beginning of an arch's spring can be seen. The arch was set on impost-blocks with large bosses (raised center portions) that are still visible. This arch apparently supported a stairway (20) that descended to the road that ran along the eastern wall. (In this, it paralleled the stairway over Robinson's Arch on the other side of the Temple Mount.) At the top of the stairway, a double doorway, also partially preserved, led into storage vaults, erroneously called Solomon's Stables. Although above street level, these vaults lay below the level of the Temple court. Perhaps wine, flour and incense for Temple rituals were stored here. The vaults were probably connected with the Triple Gate passageways, which led up to the Temple court and which were used by the priests.

---

*The devil took Jesus up to the "pinnacle of the Temple" and told him to throw himself down in order to prove he was the Son of God. Jesus replied, "It is written, 'You should not tempt the Lord your God.'"

SOUTHERN WALL SHOPS.
Burnt into the Temple Mount wall, the imprint of an arch provides a ghostly reminder of the eighth day of the Hebrew month of Elul, 70 A.D. On that day in August, Roman soldiers overran the Temple and its precincts, putting everything to the torch. This small, arched cell—probably a shop— burned along with many like it on the southern wall. This arch imprint is the first one east of the Triple Gate (see drawing, pp. 30-31).

At a point in the eastern wall, 106 feet north of the southeast corner, is a seam in the masonry—the famous "straight joint." Obviously the part of the wall south of this seam was added to the earlier wall. The masonry on the two sides of this seam are quite distinct from one another. The southern extension is clearly Herodian and is remarkably well preserved. The date of the wall north of the "straight joint" is still the subject of heated controversy.*

The location of the gate to the Temple court in the eastern wall is, as yet, undetermined. The only visible entranceway, the Golden Gate, dates from the Omayyad period (seventh century A.D.). The arch of another

---

*For one view and a review of the arguments, see Ernest-Marie Laperrousaz, "King Solomon's Wall Still Supports the Temple Mount," **BAR**, May/June 1987.

gate* lies directly beneath the blocked entranceway of the Golden Gate, but the location of this lower gate precludes its being Herodian. This lower gate is flush with the Golden Gate that is visible today. The Golden Gate protrudes from the line of the wall, so the lower gate does also. But none of the other gates of the Herodian enclosure wall around the Temple Mount protruded from the wall as this one does. In fact, gates set flush in the wall are also the rule in the other Herodian sacred precincts, such as the ones at Damascus and Hebron.

At the northeast corner of the Temple Mount, the Herodian tower (21) still stands to a considerable height. One of the original shooting holes of the tower is still visible today.

At the northwest corner of the Temple Mount stood the Antonia Fortress (22), built by Herod on the site of an earlier fortress and named after Mark Antony, the Roman commander. Josephus relates that the Antonia Fortress was built as a "guard to the Temple." Manned by a Roman legion, the fortress had a tower on each of its four corners. The southeast tower was 70 cubits high (approximately 112 feet) "and so commanded a view of the whole area of the Temple" (L., *The Jewish War* 5.5.8). Josephus tells us that the Antonia Fortress was erected on a rock 50 cubits (approximately 80 feet) high and was situated on a great precipice. Archaeologists believe it was located on the rock scarp where the Omariya School now stands. Although not a trace of the fortress itself has been found, one of the large buttresses of the fortress was revealed in the tunneling conducted along the western wall by the Ministry of Religious Affairs.

This project has also brought to light the western wall's remaining Herodian gate (23), previously discovered by Warren while tunneling under rigorous conditions. Since its original discovery by him, it has been known as Warren's Gate. Immediately to the south of this gate, the largest stones (24) in the Temple Mount have been found. They are almost 11 1/2 feet high. The largest of four especially impressive stones is 47 1/2 feet long. It weighs approximately 400 tons.

We have now made the full circuit round the Temple Mount wall. In

---

*See James Fleming, "The Undiscovered Gate Beneath Jerusalem's Golden Gate," **BAR**, January/February 1983.

THE EASTERN WALL. Preserved on this eastern side of the Temple Mount (right) are many Herodian features that mirror those on the opposite, western wall. Three windows, a double gateway and the spring of an arch set on impost blocks are all visible if you use the drawings (below) to guide your eye. Like Robinson's Arch on the western wall, the arch on the eastern wall supported a stairway that led from the Temple Mount to a road below.

Two stones to the left of the arch's spring, a strong vertical line begins, created by slight projections of the ashlars from the face of the wall. The projections gradually deepen from course to course. The vertical line thereby created on the wall was the visual continuation of the northeastern corner of a tower that once projected above the corner of the Temple Mount wall (drawing, bottom). Above the arch, a double doorway provided access to storage vaults that lay below the level of the Temple court.

Just north of the arch's spring, a "seam" extends about halfway up the wall. This seam, called the "straight joint," identifies the beginning of the Herodian expansion of the Temple Mount to the south. The seam separates smoothly dressed Herodian ashlars on the left from rough ashlars on the right belonging to the earlier wall.

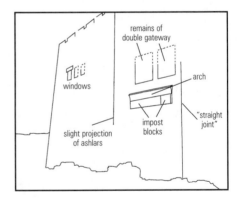

remains of double gateway

windows

arch

impost blocks

"straight joint"

slight projection of ashlars

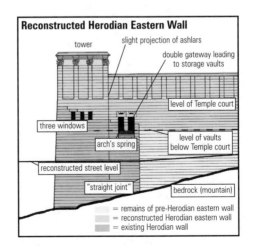

Reconstructed Herodian Eastern Wall

tower   slight projection of ashlars

double gateway leading to storage vaults

level of Temple court

three windows

arch's spring

level of vaults below Temple court

reconstructed street level

"straight joint"

bedrock (mountain)

= remains of pre-Herodian eastern wall
= reconstructed Herodian eastern wall
= existing Herodian wall

our own way, we have followed the injunction of Psalm 48:

> Walk around Zion, circle it;
> count its towers,
> take note of its ramparts;
> go through its citadels,
> that you may recount it to a future age.

We are especially indebted to the late Professor Benjamin Mazar of the Hebrew University, who always encouraged us and allowed us to publish material from the Temple Mount excavations.

2

A Pilgrim's Journey

Kathleen Ritmeyer

J erusalem is bathed in the clear light of early morning. A pilgrim has come for one of the great festivals, and his journey is almost over. He begins the ascent from the Siloam Pool at the bottom part of the Lower City (see drawing, p. 42). The sun is not yet casting its harsh glare on the stepped street paved with large limestone slabs, which is the path he must take to the Temple Mount. The pilgrim's eyes rest for a moment on the glittering spikes of the Temple in the distance; then he moves on. The houses of the Lower City are spread out before him like the crescent of the moon; higher up, on his left, he can see the magnificent palaces of the nobility in the Upper City. As he proceeds up the valley past the oldest part of the city, established by David and Solomon, he can still see, on his right, some of the splendid old palaces.

All along the street, merchants of the lower market are busy setting up their stalls for the day's business. The pilgrim is jostled by the farmers and traders who have come to buy and sell and by their beasts of burden. Baskets of luscious fruit, piles of cheeses, jars of wine and mounds of

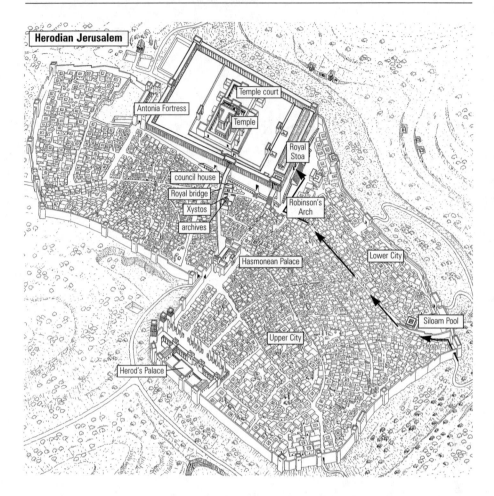

Herodian Jerusalem

Antonia Fortress

Temple court

Temple

Royal Stoa

council house

Royal bridge

Xystos

Robinson's Arch

archives

Hasmonean Palace

Lower City

Siloam Pool

Upper City

Herod's Palace

bread are set out hurriedly on rough wooden tables. The unloading of bales of richly colored silks from a wagon causes an outbreak of excitement and arguing.

At the end of this stepped street, the pilgrim comes to a busy intersection. Visitors from many lands—Ethiopians, Macedonians, Cretans, Parthians and Romans from every part of the Roman Empire—are moving toward the great plaza that fronts the monumental staircase leading up to the Double Gate of the Temple Mount. A different language from each group of people creates a cacophony of sound.

Our pilgrim climbs the first flights of the imposing staircase that leads to a gate in the western wall. The hubbub of the markets becomes fainter.

He reaches the central platform of the staircase, which affords him a fine view and an opportunity to rest. The whole of the Lower City and a large portion of the Upper City are spread out below him.

On the west, the Upper City has the appearance of an impenetrable wall, the houses are so densely packed together. The Hasmonean Palace, built before Herod's time, rises high above its surroundings, and people can be seen moving about on its roof. Looking north, he sees the archives building and the Xystos, the open-air plaza in front of the old city wall where athletic games were held during the Hellenistic period. On the other side of the plaza, opposite the Xystos, stands the elegant council house, or *bule*, whose outer walls match the walls of the Temple Mount for beauty. A procession of priests moves solemnly over the bridge that spans the Tyropoeon Valley, a bridge that gives the priests and nobles direct access from the Upper City to the Temple Mount. The thronged street below veers off to the northwest in the direction of the city gate that leads to Damascus. As far as the eye can see, the upper market is crowded with milling traders, buyers and visitors attired in strange costumes.

The pilgrim braces himself for the remaining climb up the staircase that leads to the Temple Mount. Flanked by two massive limestone pillars, so highly polished that they resemble marble, the gate evokes deep awe from the pilgrim. Looking up, he admires the gold-plated Corinthian capitals that crown the pillars. Inside the propylaeum, or gate building, the shade is refreshing. Groups of people linger, luxuriating in the respite from glare and bustle.

A different scene greets his eyes as he enters the Royal Stoa proper on the Temple Mount. A long hall, supported by four rows of thick columns stretches out in front of him. The northern side is open and leads to the Temple court. Long shafts of dust-flecked sunlight are filtered through the windows in the upper part of the stoa and glance off a scene of frenzied commercial activity. At the tables of the money changers, the pilgrim exchanges coins bearing the image of Caesar for silver shekels without the forbidden graven image. Women who have recently given birth are crowded at the stalls nearby, haggling over the price of the doves and pigeons they will sacrifice in gratitude for the happy conclusions of their pregnancies. Those who successfully complete a purchase walk away bearing small cages. Oxen and sheep for sacrifices are also offered for sale; the smell of their droppings permeates the entire area.

At the eastern end of the portico is a partition through which members of the Sanhedrin are emerging after a session. The pilgrim observes on the other side of the partition the beauty of the apse specially constructed to accommodate the Sanhedrin. A magnificent stone arch covered with a rich variety of geometric and floral patterns forms the backdrop for the Sanhedrin conferences. The tiers of smooth stone steps on which they sit while conferring are now empty.

Leaving behind the noise of the cooing doves and the bleating animals, the pilgrim moves on and passes through the open portico in the direction of the Temple. Soon, merging with the crowds pouring out of the underground stairway leading up from the Double Gate, he becomes part of the great throng who have come to worship at the "House of the Lord."

3

Quarrying and Transporting Stones for Herod's Temple Mount

Leen Ritmeyer

Herod's construction in the Temple Mount area, like the construction of most of Jerusalem's buildings, used local limestone. The mountains around Jerusalem are composed of Turonian and Cenomanian limestone that has a characteristic horizontal layering. These horizontal layers vary between about 18 inches and 5 feet thick. In exceptional cases, the layers are even thicker.

To quarry this limestone the stonecutter first straightened the face of the stone. This consisted of chiseling the rock in such a way as to produce a flat vertical surface—the side of the incipient stone—and a flat surface on top. Next, with a pickaxe he dug narrow channels 4 to 6 inches wide on all sides except the bottom of the incipient stone. In two of these grooves, at right angles, the quarryman would insert dry wooden beams, hammer them tightly into place and pour water over them. This caused the wood to swell, and the consequent pressure caused the stone to separate from the lower rock layer.

The next stage required squaring off the stones and preparing them

***STONE
QUARRYING***
*in Herod's time
(above). A stone-
cutter, right, uses
a pickaxe to cut
a channel in a
limestone block.
Meanwhile another
worker, left, pours
water over some
logs stacked in the
channel between
two blocks. The
water will cause
the wood to swell,
exerting lateral
pressure on the
block and splitting
the block off of
the bedrock to*

HERSHEL SHANKS

*which it is attached at bottom. Because the limestone lay in natural horizontal layers the blocks
would cleave along a relatively neat, horizontal line.*

*Remains of an ancient quarrying operation (above) can be seen at a tomb complex near the Siloam
Pool. Shallow, incomplete channels cut around incipient blocks appear in the bedrock.*

for transportation. The smaller stones were simply placed on wagons, according to Josephus. Some of the corner stones in the Temple Mount, however, weighed 50 tons or more. Special techniques were developed to transport these stones on large wooden rollers. While shaping the stones, the masons left 12-inch-long projections on opposite sides of each stone. These projections were later removed. In the meantime, ropes were placed around these projections, and two short, strong cranes outfitted with winches lifted the stones on one side and lowered them onto rollers. Oxen could then pull the stones with ropes placed around the projections.

MOVING THE STONES. Stages of quarrying and moving ashlars (below). In the background, at left, the unworked bedrock exhibits the natural horizontal layering of the limestone in the Jerusalem vicinity. Blocks cut, but not yet removed, appear at upper right. The thickness of the limestone layers determined the height of the blocks that were quarried.

At lower left, a stonecutter dresses some rough blocks, taking care to leave projections on opposite sides of each block. The finished product, an ashlar with a projection and margins on its outer face, lies to his right.

Ropes are looped around the stone projections. Using a crane, lower right, a foreman supervises as the crane hoists one end of the block off the ground and lowers it upon a wooden roller.

At center, an ashlar begins its journey out of the quarry. Hitched to the stone by ropes looped around the projections, a team of oxen pulls the block. Wooden rollers ease the ashlar's movement. As the ashlar inches forward, rollers left behind at the rear are moved to the front.

BUILDING THE WALL. *Building Herod's Temple Mount wall involved several steps, as illustrated in this drawing (below). First the line of the wall was laid out by markers (1). Then the construction site was cleared down to bedrock (2). Next the bedrock itself had to be cut and leveled before the ashlars could be put into place (3). Oxen hauled the ashlars from the quarry on rollers (4) for a mile or so down to the construction site, which was 125 feet lower than the quarries north of the Temple Mount. A crane powered by a treadmill lowered the blocks into place (5), and once the courses had been laid, workers chiseled off the projections (6). In a few cases, a projection was not chiseled off for some reason, as this example from the southeast corner shows (left), thus providing archaeologists with excellent evidence of the construction process.*

Herod's builders solved the problem of how to hoist huge ashlars onto a rising wall. They worked from inside the wall. At the completion of each course of ashlars, the area within the retaining wall was filled in, up to the top of the latest course, with cartloads of "hard core" (7), which consists of broken stones and rubble such as quarry chips. Thus a new working level for the next course was created that allowed the stones to be moved into place with minimal lifting by the crane.

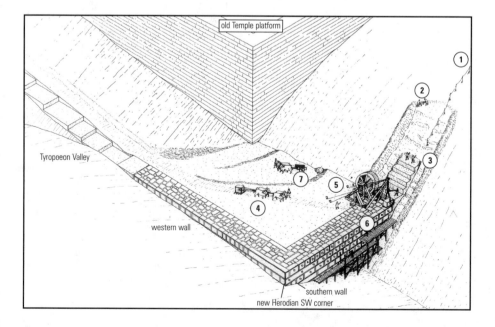

old Temple platform

Tyropoeon Valley

western wall

southern wall
new Herodian SW corner

According to Josephus, 1,000 oxen were used in this work.

The quarries were probably located near what we know today as the Russian Compound, in the heart of modern Jerusalem. A 50-foot-long column, still attached to the bedrock, can be seen there. In the process of quarrying the column, a natural fissure was observed in the rock, so the workmen simply left the damaged column in place. The quarries in this area are 125 feet higher than the Temple Mount, so the journey of over a mile to the Temple Mount was downhill. Using the force of gravity obviously made transportation easier.

Once the stones arrived at the building site, they had to be put in place. At both the southwest and southeast corners of the Temple Mount, stones weighing over 80 tons are still in place at a height of at least 100 feet above the foundations. How did they get there? At our excavation site, some of the more pious local laborers who worked with these stones were so awed by their size that they attributed their placement to angels. It would have been impossible, they said, for mere men to lift them into place. In a sense, they were right; no man could have lifted these stones to such a height, notwithstanding all the sophisticated Roman engineering equipment available at the time.

In fact, the stones did not have to be lifted from below. They were actually lowered into place from above. The 16-foot-thick walls of the Temple Mount are basically retaining walls, built to retain the high pressure of the fill that was dumped between the previous platform and the new Temple Mount wall. This was Herod's way of enlarging the previous platform to twice its original size. Herod's engineers solved the construction problem by pouring the internal fill simultaneously with the construction of the walls. Thus, the first course of stones was laid in the valley surrounding the previous Temple Mount. Then the area between the new and old walls was filled up to the level of the top of this course. This created a new work level on top of which, from the inside, a second course of stones could be laid. Again fill would be added on the inside, so that a third course of stones could be laid. And so on, course after course, until the whole of Herod's extension was raised up to the level of the previous Temple platform.

The buildings on the Temple Mount were built of smaller stones. Stones from these structures were thrown down into the street below when the Romans destroyed Jerusalem in 70 A.D. Most of them were later scavenged for other construction. But a few were found in the excavations. These weighed between two and three tons. Stones of this size would have posed no problem for the skilled builders of Herod's Temple Mount.

4

RECONSTRUCTING THE TRIPLE GATE

Leen and Kathleen Ritmeyer

Reconstructing the Triple Gate required that we answer three principal questions: What was the gate's original width? Was it originally a double gate or a triple gate? For whom was it built? The discovery of a vault in front of the Triple Gate—about 23 feet south of the facade—gave us critical information for understanding the gateway in its earliest form. A vault is a wide arch that forms the roof or ceiling of a chamber. This vault supported a stairway leading up to the Triple Gate. (A stairway was required in order to ascend from the plaza to the threshold of the Triple Gate; some of the steps from this stairway were actually found in the excavation.) The width of the vault provided us with the width of the stairway leading up to the gate. Although the vault is only about three-quarters preserved, it is easily reconstructed on the basis of symmetry. The west side of the vault aligns perfectly with the west door jamb of the Triple Gate. (This door jamb with its beautiful molding is the only original element of the Triple Gate exterior that has survived. Additional Herodian construction is evident

TRIPLE GATE. *The arches of the Triple Gate (left) have been sealed since the gate was rebuilt in the seventh century A.D. A two-chambered vault excavated below and in front of the Triple Gate shows us the gate's original width exactly. This vault supported a stairway that led up to the Triple Gate.*

A narrow wall separated the two chambers of the vault (plan, below). Remains of this narrow wall are visible below and just right of the center of the middle gate of the Triple Gate. The chamber to the left of this dividing wall has survived intact and enables us to calculate, with the assumption of symmetry, the measurements of the right-hand chamber. The total width of the two chambers and dividing wall give us the width of the Herodian stairway and, thus, of the Triple Gate.

The only Herodian element of the Triple Gate still preserved stands at the end of a row of Herodian ashlars that extends from the center left edge of the photo to the base of the left arch of the Triple Gate. The last ashlar in this row, abutting the Triple Gate, displays fine vertical molding and originally was part of the gate's door jamb (see the reconstruction of the Temple Mount southern wall, pp. 30-31).

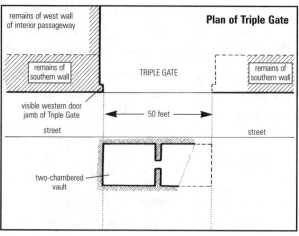

Plan of Triple Gate

remains of west wall
of interior passageway

remains of
southern wall

TRIPLE GATE

remains of
southern wall

visible western door
jamb of Triple Gate

◄— 50 feet —►

street

street

two-chambered
vault

inside the gate. The present-day western wall of the passageway that originally led from the gate up to the Temple court (as in the Double Gate) is constructed on bedrock foundation. One Herodian column base is still visible within the gateway. This column base is a double-width pilaster, that is, a column attached to and protruding from a wall.) A narrow wall divides the vault in front of the Triple Gate into two chambers. We know the width of the eastern chamber from the width of the preserved western chamber. The total width of the vault is 50 feet.

The width of the vault, as we said, tells us the width of the stairway and this, in turn, tells us the width of the Triple Gate to which the stairway led. We confirmed our reasoning when we observed that the width we were assigning to this gateway was identical to the width of the gates that stood over Robinson's Arch and Wilson's Arch on the western wall of the Temple Mount.

The blocked Triple Gate visible today is of Omayyad (seventh century A.D.) construction, but its width reflects the original dimensions of the Herodian gate. But was this gate originally a triple gate? Or was it a double gate? We assume that even originally it was a triple gate—for two reasons: (1) at 50 feet, it is considerably wider than the 39-foot-wide Double Gate (in the southern wall, to the west of the Triple Gate); (2) classical gates were, with only few exceptions, either single or triple—and clearly 50 feet is too wide for a single gate.

The Mishnah tells us that there were "two Hulda gates at the south, serving for entry and exit" (*Middot* 1:3). Scholars and exegetes have long argued over whether the two Hulda gates referred to in this passage were the Double Gate and the Triple Gate or, on the other hand, the two passages of the Double Gate. Some say pilgrims went in one side of the Double Gate and came out the other. Others would have the pilgrims going in via the Double Gate and coming out via the Triple Gate (or vice versa).

Our view is that the Mishnah refers to the two passages through the Double Gate and that pilgrims entered through one passage and exited from the other. Let us explain why.

First, as we have already noted, the Double Gate has a very broad—210 foot—staircase leading up to it; the staircase leading up to the Triple Gate is much narrower—50 feet. Second, as we have also noted, a double gate is a rare phenomenon in classical architecture. When found—for example, at the Porta Negra in Trier, Germany—it always involves the circulation of two-way traffic: one side for going in and the other for going out. Third, the Double Gate opens into a passageway that led directly up and onto the Temple court. The Triple Gate also had a ramp that gave access to the Temple court, but it seems to have been more directly connected with the underground vaulted storerooms that are today quite erroneously called Solomon's Stables.

What did the Triple Gate originally look like? Unfortunately, so little of the Herodian construction of this gate has been preserved that we have little guidance in reconstructing it.* However, we believe we have located a parallel to the Triple Gate—described below—which may tell us what the gate looked like. Features of this parallel structure also suggest that the Triple Gate had a priestly function. (For this reason, too, we believe that the Double Gate was used by ordinary pilgrims.)

Josephus tells us (*The Jewish War* 5.12.2) about a tomb complex built for the family of the high priest Ananias. It seems, from Josephus's description, that the tomb complex was located near the Siloam Pool, where the Hinnom Valley leads into the Kidron Valley. In the early part of this century, remains of a splendid tomb complex were investigated in this area—near where the Monastery of St. Onuphrius now stands. This investigation was undertaken first by the Irish archaeologist R.A.S. Macalister[1] and then by the German scholar Knut Olaf Dalman.[2] This area is some distance from the Temple Mount, so it escaped the horrible destruction inflicted by the Romans in 70 A.D. Only fragments of architectural elements have been found in the Temple Mount area. By contrast, here at the mouth of the Hinnom Valley, magnificent Herodian remains still stand to their full

---

*In our earlier reconstructions, we drew only a single building in this area—a bathhouse—between the Double and Triple Gates. But this was only a tentative decision. With the discovery of a drainage channel (a feature usually found under Herodian streets) running south through this area, we concluded that a stepped street must have separated the area between the two gates into a western and an eastern half, with separate buildings on either side. This called for a new interpretation of the function of these buildings between the Double and Triple Gates—buildings that were heavily reconstructed in later times. The building west of the stepped street, now drawn at a considerably reduced size from our original reconstructions, was designated as a *mikveh* (ritual bathhouse) for purification before entering the sanctuary. Locating one of the courts of law east of the stepped street provides a very probable solution to the puzzle of the function of the rest of the building complex.

TOMBS RESEMBLING THE TRIPLE GATE. *In clear view of the Triple Gate, an elegant Herodian-style tomb complex (right) may be the burial place of the family of Ananias, high priest of the Temple. The tomb may have been carved to resemble the Triple Gate, through which priests entered and departed the Temple precincts. Many architectural elements of this tomb complex survive intact, giving us examples, perhaps even artistic duplicates, of the proportions and decorations of the Triple Gate.*

The darkened doorway to a burial chamber pierces the back wall of the tomb's anteroom (upper right).

Projecting forward above the doorway, remains of the front wall of the anteroom display a seashell decoration. Originally a full semicircle, this seashell was carved above the central entrance of a now-destroyed triple gate to this tomb anteroom (reconstruction drawing, above). In the reconstruction of the Temple Mount's Triple Gate (p. 31), author Ritmeyer used the proportions of this tomb's triple gate as a model. However, he varied the styles of the three doorways to reflect examples in the tomb complex and excavated remains.

Instead of a seashell over the central entrance of the Triple Gate, Ritmeyer drew a pediment. One of these pediments appears in the tomb complex, above an Attic mock-doorway (center of middle photo). The opening in the lower part of this doorway is a burial niche. Above the three burial niches, a scalloped dome mimics the domes inside the Double Gate (see p. 35). The side entrances in the Temple Mount Triple Gate are modeled after Attic doorways without pediments (bottom photo), which were found in the tomb complex and also were found as architectural fragments scattered around the Temple Mount walls.

height. The decoration used in this tomb complex closely resembles what we see on the fragments from the Temple Mount excavations. We believe many elements in these tombs, which—as Professor Benjamin Mazar pointed out to us—are in view of the Triple Gate, duplicate elements of the gates to the Temple.

One particular tomb is especially noteworthy. A triple gate cut out of the bedrock originally provided the entrance to the anteroom of this tomb. The proportions of the triple gate in the facade of this tomb seem to have been a kind of miniature of the Triple Gate in the southern wall of the Temple Mount. It seems likely that a priestly family built this tomb. Perhaps they wanted to transfer to their last resting place some of the magnificence they were accustomed to seeing as they approached the Temple court from the Triple Gate.

Inside the tomb, the chambers, like others in this complex, have side-molding that closely corresponds to the molding of the western jamb of the Triple Gate.

In our reconstruction of the Temple Mount's Triple Gate, we have used the proportions of the tomb's triple gate and the side-molding found inside many of these tombs to outline the doorways in the Temple Mount's Triple Gate. We have reconstructed the style of the three entrances as Attic doorways, based on the Attic doorways found in these tombs. (We also found fragments of Attic doorways in the Temple Mount excavations.) The molding on the lintel of Attic doorways extends beyond the jambs (see photo, p. 55, bottom). Finally, in our reconstruction of the Temple Mount Triple Gate, we have placed a pediment over the center entrance, just as we found it on three Attic mock-doorways inside the tomb.

Putting all the evidence together, we now conclude that the narrower stairway leading to the Triple Gate was used by the priests. The magnificent broad stairway leading to the Double Gate was trod by pilgrims on their way up to, and down from, the Temple Mount. But the facade of the Triple Gate—the priests' gate—was far more elaborate than the undecorated facade of the Double Gate—the gate of the masses.

5

LOCATING THE
ORIGINAL TEMPLE MOUNT

Leen Ritmeyer

S omewhere on Jerusalem's majestic Temple Mount—the largest man-made platform in the ancient world, nearly 145 acres— Herod the Great (37-4 B.C.) built a new Temple to the Israelite God, Yahweh, doubtless on the very spot where the exiles returning from Babylonia more than 500 years earlier had rebuilt the original Temple, first erected in the tenth century B.C. by King Solomon. But where was that spot?

Efforts to locate it have relied on clues from archaeological evidence on the Mount itself and from two famous descriptions of Herod's Temple— one by the first-century A.D. Jewish historian, Josephus, and the other in a tractate of the Mishnah called *Middot*. All these efforts to locate the site of the Temple have foundered, however, on the seemingly contradictory descriptions of Josephus and *Middot* and on the paucity of archaeological clues.

But all have focused on elements of the Temple, rather than on the Temple Mount. I would like to try a different approach. I would like to

BARON WOLMAN

BASKING IN JERUSALEM'S LUMINOUS LIGHT, the Temple Mount and the Old City of *Jerusalem reflect the early morning sun in a view toward the northwest. Today dominated by the golden Dome of the Rock (center) and the silver-domed El-Aqsa mosque (lower left), two of the holiest shrines in Islam, the Temple Mount was—until the Roman destruction of Jerusalem in 70 A.D.—the site of ancient Israel's holy Temple.*

The size of 30 football fields, the nearly rectangular Temple Mount attained its current size and shape during an ambitious expansion program begun by King Herod in 19 B.C. The Dome of the Rock sits on a smaller, somewhat trapezoidal raised area referred to as the Muslim Platform. The First Temple and the Second Temple as rebuilt by the returning exiles stood on a square Temple Mount somewhere within the borders of the current Temple Mount. Until now, no one knew for sure just where this early Temple Mount was located. Now author Leen Ritmeyer, formerly architect for the Temple Mount excavations begun after 1967 under the direction of Hebrew University Professor Benjamin Mazar, has pieced together subtle archaeological clues to convincingly locate the original Temple Mount and to make a highly persuasive suggestion on the location of the Temple itself.

reverse the process—first to locate the Temple Mount in various periods and only then—and at present, only tentatively—to place the Temple on the Temple Mount during each period.

As previously mentioned, Herod the Great approximately doubled the size of the Temple Mount by extending the earlier Temple Mount on the north, south and west. He could not extend it on the east because the land drops off steeply to the Kidron Valley beyond the wall on that side.

But where was the earlier Temple Mount, the one repaired by Nehemiah to create a level area on which to rebuild the Temple to the Lord? I believe we can now—for the first time—locate the Temple Mount of the First Temple period with considerable confidence.

The demonstration will rely on clues still visible on the site, on the text of Josephus and the tractate *Middot*, and especially on the work of the greatest underground explorer of Jerusalem of all times—Captain (later Sir) Charles Warren.

A brilliant engineer for the London-based Palestine Exploration Fund, Warren conducted investigations in Jerusalem between 1867-1870. His work followed the comprehensive survey and mapping of Jerusalem by Captain (later Colonel, then Sir) Charles Wilson, an engineer with the British Army who subsequently collaborated with Warren to bring out the *Recovery of Jerusalem* in 1871. In it we have a faithful record of the mysterious caverns, caves, tunnels and cisterns that lie underground, beneath the Temple Mount.[1]

Although others, such as the British Captain Claude Conder and the German architect Conrad Schick, also involved themselves with the exploration of the cisterns beneath the Temple Mount, the work of Warren, carried out while he was still in his twenties, stands as a landmark of systematic investigation and painstaking accuracy. Together with his faithful assistant, Sergeant Henry Birtles, and some local workmen, he surveyed 36 of the 37 underground structures, not to mention the extensive series of shafts and tunnels he dug outside, along the retaining walls of the Temple Mount, to assist his explorations.

One well-known scholar of Jerusalem's archaeology has described Warren's unique achievement this way:

> The great album of *Plans, Elevations, Sections, etc.* registering his results, is an accomplishment ... unequalled in the annals of Palestinian archaeology in its grandiose scale and sumptuous execution. Moreover, Warren's explanatory records, especially his *Recovery of Jerusalem*, shows that every measurement and every drawing is the result of unheard of exertions and great courage.[2]

A quotation from Warren's own record of his exploration of cistern 17 (see plan, p. 71) will help explain why, as noted in the preface to the *Recovery of Jerusalem*, he returned to England in ill health, suffering from fever and exhaustion:

> On sounding I found it 42 feet down to water. I tried to descend, but to no purpose, until I had nearly stripped to the skin and even then in my contortions I managed to slip the rope over one arm ... On getting down to the water I found it only 3 feet deep and concluding from the size of the cistern that help would be required in measuring, I signaled for Sergeant Birtles to come down ... In the meantime the excitement of our "find" had begun to wear off and the water felt cold. I was just giving the sergeant some sage advice as to how he could direct his steps to the best advantage, when I stumbled over a large stone and fell into the water flat on my face. As just at present the weather is frosty and the rain is generally accompanied by sleet or hail, a bath in one's clothes is anything but pleasant ... We were altogether three hours in the water measuring and I took everything I could get at and have put the most important measurements on the 10 feet to an inch plan.[3]

My own interest in tracing the development of the Temple Mount goes back to 1973 when I began work as field architect to the Hebrew University archaeological expedition directed by Professor Benjamin Mazar, which was excavating south and southwest of the Temple Mount. Mazar, who died in 1995, was the doyen of Israeli archaeologists. He had an uncanny intellectual intuition and an extraordinary knowledge of the archaeological as well as historical sources. I remember the moment well: Mazar and I were sitting in his room at the Hebrew University in the spring of 1980. He was reading a passage from Nehemiah 2:8 that referred to "beams for the gates of the *birah* that related to the Temple."

"What and where is the *birah*?" Mazar asked.

Little did I suspect that this question would eventually lead to a breakthrough in the understanding of the architectural development of the Temple Mount.

WHERE'S THE SQUARE? How did Leen Ritmeyer locate the original Temple Mount platform? This plan highlights the clues he used to identify each corner of the square structure. Unlike earlier researchers, who started with their understanding of where the Temple stood and then tried to outline the platform around it, Ritmeyer first assembled archaeological clues to pinpoint the square Temple platform. Only then did he venture to locate the Temple itself.

1. THE TELLTALE "STEP"

Ritmeyer noted two anomalies about the bottom step of the staircase at the northwest corner of the platform: it consists of pre-Herodian building blocks and it is parallel not to the Muslim Platform but to the eastern wall of the Temple Mount. Ritmeyer wondered if this step was actually part of an early wall. He also noted that a line drawn to the east from the northern edge of these blocks passes along a rock scarp (a sheared-off rock ledge) before meeting the eastern wall. The length of this line is 861 feet, equal to 500 royal cubits by the 20.67 inches-per-cubit measure. Five hundred cubits is the measurement given in an ancient Jewish source for each side of the Temple platform.

2. THE NORTHERN PART OF THE EASTERN WALL

Ritmeyer noticed another anomaly at his postulated northeast Temple Mount corner. The lowest course above ground in this area protrudes from the later and clearly different masonry above it. This protruding course ends at the point marked offset on the plan, north of the northeastern corner of the proposed square Temple Mount. Ritmeyer hypothesized that a defensive tower stood in the area between the northeast corner of the square Temple Mount and the offset. A comparable tower may have been attached at the northwest corner, between the "step" and the fosse, or moat.

3. THE SOUTHERN END OF THE EASTERN WALL

A slight bend in the eastern wall helped Ritmeyer fix the southeastern corner of the Temple Mount. The famous 19th-century explorer of Jerusalem, Charles Warren, recorded this bend. When Ritmeyer measured it he found that it began exactly 500 royal cubits south of where his proposed northern wall intersects the eastern wall. Ritmeyer then drew a perpendicular line west from where the bend in the eastern wall begins and a line directly south from the "step," yielding two sides each 500 cubits long. Later expansions of this original square platform, as Ritmeyer reconstructs them, are shown on pp. 65-67; his placement of the Temple appears on pp. 64 and 86.

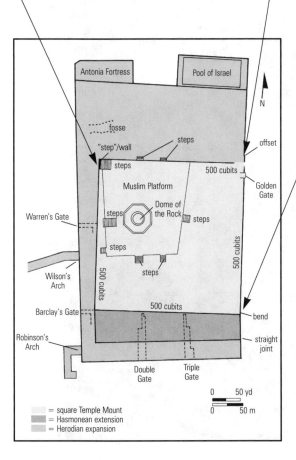

Antonia Fortress

Pool of Israel

N

fosse

"step"/wall

steps

offset

steps

500 cubits

Muslim Platform

Golden Gate

Dome of the Rock

Warren's Gate

steps

steps

steps

500 cubits

steps

Wilson's Arch

500 cubits

steps

Barclay's Gate

500 cubits

bend

Robinson's Arch

straight joint

Double Gate

Triple Gate

0   50 yd
0   50 m

= square Temple Mount
= Hasmonean extension
= Herodian expansion

THE TELLTALE "STEP." The unobtrusive stone blocks (right) at the foot of a staircase (bottom) leading to the northwest corner of the Muslim Platform on which the Dome of the Rock now sits (see plan, previous page) are the keys to locating the original square Temple Mount. Though these stones look like the bottom step of the staircase, a careful examination of the southernmost stone of the step before its front side was completely covered (photo below) revealed a margin and the boss of an ashlar block. What looked like a bottom step was, in fact, a wall of ashlars. The width of the margin and the protrusion of the boss identified the ashlar—and, therefore, the wall of which it was a part—as pre-Herodian. The recent paving by Muslim authorities (far right in the photo at right), level with the top surface of this lowest step, has obscured the margin and boss on the side of the stone.

My first reaction to his question was to suggest that the *birah*, often mistranslated as palace, might be synonymous with the 500-square-cubit measurement given for the Temple Mount in *Middot* 2:1.

"So," Mazar followed up, "where is this square?"

It would have been helpful if we could have asked Charles Warren to join our "think tank," but although this was not possible we did have in our office his album of *Plans, Elevations, Sections, etc.* which contains detailed plans of the underground structures of the Temple Mount.[4] Armed with this and Mazar's knowledge of the historical sources, we set out to discover the location of this square Temple Mount.

The preliminary results were announced by Professor Mazar at the First International Congress on Biblical Archaeology held in Jerusalem in April 1984. The proposed square-shaped Temple Mount was promptly dubbed the "Ritmeyer Square."[5]

I have continued to study the architectural development of the Temple Mount and believe that it is now possible to demonstrate the results in more detail and with greater confidence.

The demonstration begins with a flight of steps leading up from the Temple Mount to the Muslim Platform, the raised area on which the Dome of the Rock is built. Eight flights of steps lead up to the platform on which the Dome of the Rock sits; at the top of each flight of steps is an arcade that marks architecturally the entrance to the Muslim Platform.

One of these flights of steps is different, however—the one at the northwest corner. Each of the others is parallel to the wall of the Muslim Platform where it rises; that is, the bottom step of each staircase is parallel to the wall of the Muslim Platform and this determines the direction of the flight of steps.

However, the bottom step of the flight at the northwestern corner of the Muslim Platform is not exactly parallel to the wall to which it leads. This was pointed out to me in 1972 by my predecessor at the Temple Mount excavations, the Irish architect Brian Lalor. Each higher step on this flight of steps is naturally parallel to the lowest one, so the whole flight of steps is a bit off—that is, not exactly parallel to the wall to which it leads. Moreover, the construction of the bottom step is also different. It is made of a single line of large ashlars (rectangular blocks of hewn

HOW THE TEMPLE MOUNT DEVELOPED. The four major stages of development of the Temple Mount platform shown here and on the next three pages are viewed as plans seen from above and as perspective reconstructions viewed from the southwest.

SQUARE TEMPLE MOUNT. A square platform supported the First Temple, which was destroyed by the Babylonian ruler Nebuchadnezzar in 587/586 B.C. and then rebuilt by Nehemiah and those returning from the Babylonian Exile in about 444 B.C. According to Nehemiah 3:1 and 12:39, the towers of Hananeel and Mea stood at the northwest corner of the Temple Mount. The Sheep Gate and Prison Gate were to the east of them. As recorded in Jeremiah 31:38 and Zechariah 14:10, Hananeel existed already at the end of the First Temple period, which also indicates that the square Temple Mount existed then as well. After the destruction of Hananeel and Mea in 587/586 B.C., they were rebuilt and renamed Baris by the Hasmonean ruler John Hyrcanus I (134-104 B.C.). According to Josephus, the Baris stood on the north side of the Temple, apparently on the same spot where previously the towers of Hananeel and Mea stood. This Baris was destroyed in 63 B.C. by Pompey. Herod rebuilt Baris between 37 and 31 B.C. (that is, before he enlarged the Temple Mount) and renamed it Antonia after his patron Mark Antony. This original Antonia was located therefore at the northwest corner of the square Temple Mount. Herod later built another fortress, also called Antonia, at the northwest corner of his enlarged Temple Mount.

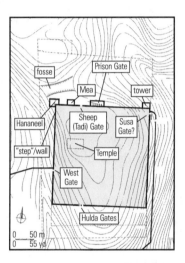

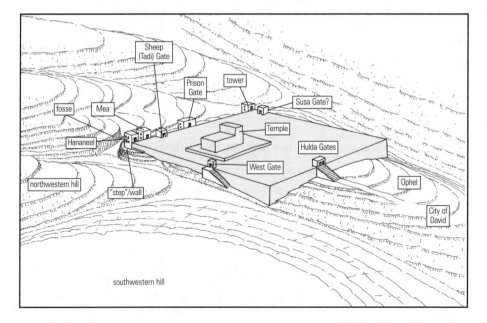

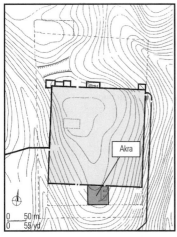

SELEUCID ADDITION. *In 186 B.C. the Seleucid ruler of Syria built the Akra, a fortress intended to control the population of Jerusalem. It adjoined the southern side of the Temple platform.*

stone) in contrast to the other steps of this flight, which are made up of many smaller stones. The southernmost ashlar had at the time a visible margin and boss on its front face. Lalor had suggested that this bottom step might be the remains of an early ashlar-built wall, which was why it was not parallel to the wall of the Muslim Platform.

After my talk with Mazar, I returned to this flight of steps and decided that the telltale lower step was a logical starting point for my continued investigation.

On this visit, I noticed something else about this bottom step composed of ashlars: It was exactly parallel to the eastern wall of the Temple Mount

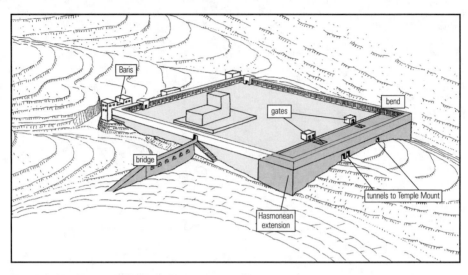

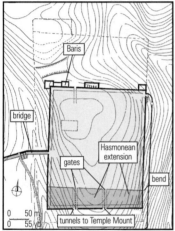

HASMONEAN EXTENSION. *The Hasmoneans extended the platform along the southern end of the Temple Mount in 141 B.C., building atop the dismantled Akra. A pair of tunnels that would later be known as the Double and Triple Gate passageways were built at the south, leading up to the mount.*

itself. When Herod enlarged the Temple Mount, he did not change the line of the eastern wall (the steep slope of the Kidron Valley was too close to the existing wall to move it). So the line of the eastern wall was pre-Herodian—perhaps even Solomonic. And now I had a wall, the lowest step on this flight of steps, that was exactly parallel to the eastern wall. I also noted that the northern end of the northernmost large stone of this step was exactly in line with the northern edge of the raised Muslim Platform.

On that later visit to the flight of steps, the sides of the ashlars that comprised the lowest step were no longer visible. The level of the adjoining pavement had been raised, concealing the sides of the ashlars. But in the office we had an early photograph that showed the boss of one of the ashlars. The boss is the central part of the ashlar that sticks out, in contrast to the margin—the edge—that encloses the boss. From the photograph, we could determine that the margin was 3.9 inches wide and the boss protruded approximately 3.1 inches. This is quite different from the typical Herodian masonry on the Temple Mount, which has a narrow margin of about 3.1 to 3.9 inches and a flat central boss that barely protrudes .4 inches. Accordingly, the ashlar in this step/wall gave a strong impression of being pre-Herodian. It looked very much like the lowest masonry in the central section of the eastern wall of the Temple Mount,

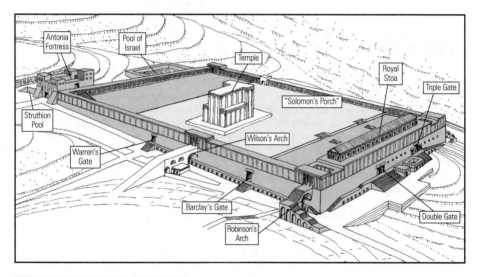

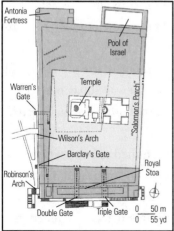

HERODIAN EXPANSION. *The last and most extensive expansion of the Temple Mount occurred under King Herod (37-4 B.C.), who enlarged the mount on the north and west and even further to the south.*

At the northwest corner of the newly expanded platform, Herod built the Antonia Fortress to defend the Temple precincts. The north side of the Temple was most vulnerable to attack because it did not have a valley to hamper assaults, as did the other three sides. Because the eastern edge of the Temple Mount drops off steeply into the Kidron Valley, no extension was ever made on that side.

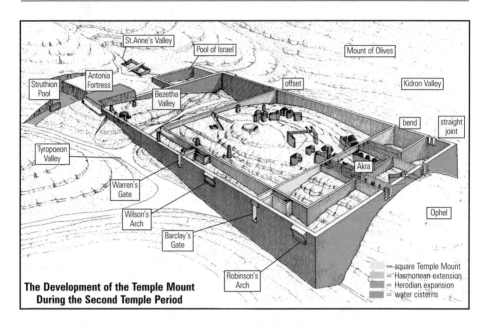

The Development of the Temple Mount During the Second Temple Period

A CUTAWAY LOOK AT THE TEMPLE MOUNT. Combining architectural features from various periods, the underlying topography of the bedrock and cisterns and passageways cut into the bedrock, this drawing shows the Temple Mount's expanding boundaries over time (in practice, older walls would have been covered over or their stones reused elsewhere when new construction took place). Not shown is the surface of the Temple Mount itself or the structures built atop it, most notably the Temple.

At center are the walls of the square Temple Mount of the First Temple period, measuring 500 cubits on each side. Extending to the south is the location of the Seleucid fortress known as the Akra, built in about 186 B.C. The Akra was dismantled in 141 B.C. and a Hasmonean addition was then built across the entire southern side of the previous square Temple Mount. The outermost walls represent the Herodian addition on the south, west and north.

near the Golden Gate. I therefore proposed that this step was actually a section of a wall—part of the western wall of the pre-Herodian, perhaps First Temple-period, Temple Mount.

If so, we had the eastern line and the western line of the pre-Herodian Temple Mount. And from *Middot*, we know that it was 500 cubits *square*. The next question was how far north and south did the original western wall extend?

For the northern end of the western wall, we turned to Warren for clues.

According to Warren's records, he discovered an "excavated ditch," 52 feet north of the step/wall we have been discussing.[6] It had been "excavated" to create a fosse, or dry moat. Mazar immediately concluded that this must have been the moat described by Strabo, the Greek historian and geographer (64 B.C.-21 A.D.), who gives its measurements as 60 feet deep and 250 feet wide.[7] The purpose of this moat could easily be surmised: The Temple Mount was protected by natural valleys on three sides, but not on the north. This moat protected the pre-Herodian Temple Mount on the north. It links the Tyropoeon Valley on the west with a branch of the Bezetha Valley[8] that runs into the Kidron Valley on the east. An enemy's approach to the Temple Mount from the north over the narrow saddle that previously existed was thus effectively cut off by the moat. Incidentally, this same moat or fosse, we are told by Josephus,[9] was filled in by Pompey's soldiers in 63 B.C. to enable the Romans to storm the towers built onto the pre-Herodian northern wall of the Temple Mount.

It was thus clear that the western wall of the pre-Herodian Temple Mount terminated on the north no more than 52 feet north of the step/wall; for that is where the moat or fosse begins. The northern wall must be south of this fosse.

With this in mind we proceeded to look for possible remains of the pre-Herodian northern Temple Mount wall. Again the trail was illuminated by Warren. Underground structure 29 on Warren's plan (see p. 71) is a vaulted passage built against the northern edge of the Muslim Platform. The southern wall of this chamber is the northern wall of the Muslim Platform. Warren described the southern wall of this chamber as a "quarried rockscarp." (The chamber, incidentally, may have been part of the Monastery of the Temple, built by the Crusaders.[10]) This rock scarp features prominently on Warren's plans.[11] We believe this scarp was cut to hold the foundation for the northern wall of the pre-Herodian Temple Mount.

A line projecting westward from this rock scarp forms a right-angled corner with the step/wall. As the northern edge of the northernmost large stone of the step/wall is exactly in line with the northern edge of the raised Muslim Platform, it follows that this large stone forms the actual northwestern corner of the pre-Herodian square Temple Mount!

The 52 feet between the northern wall and the fosse is just enough room to construct the towers described by Josephus; thus, this location of the northern wall of the pre-Herodian Temple Mount fits well with our historical information.[12]

Continuing the line of the rock scarp eastward, we can locate the northeast corner of the pre-Herodian Temple Mount at the point where it meets the eastern wall, again forming a right-angled corner, just north of the Golden Gate. It is interesting to note that the earliest type of masonry (visible in the lowest courses) in the eastern wall is to be seen at this point.

The length of the northern wall of the pre-Herodian Temple Mount (measured along the rock scarp) located between the step/wall and the present-day eastern wall of the Temple Mount is 861 feet. According to *Middot*, the pre-Herodian Temple Mount was 500 cubits on a side. There are, however, at least three kinds of cubits. For two of them, 861 feet does not make 500 cubits. But for the so-called royal cubit of 20.67 inches,[13] it turns out that 861 feet is exactly 500 cubits.

Naturally, in order to complete the 500-cubit-square Temple Mount referred to in *Middot*, we quickly measured 861 feet south from the point on the eastern wall that we had identified as the northeastern corner of the pre-Herodian Temple Mount. Here there is a slight bend in the wall, as recorded by Warren.*

To understand this bend and its significance we must look at the eastern wall more closely, assisted, of course, by the records of Warren. Beginning at the southeast corner of Herod's—that is, today's—Temple Mount, we see that the first 106 feet is clearly all Herodian masonry (see pp. 78-79). At that point there is a "straight joint," or seam, indicating where Herodian masonry was added to a pre-existing eastern wall. North of the "straight joint," on the eastern wall, is a distinctly different masonry that has been identified as characteristic of the Hasmonean period (142-37 B.C.).

Warren dug a shaft down along the eastern wall of the Temple Mount near the southeast corner and then began tunneling north. He tunneled 53 feet north of the "straight joint." On the side of his tunnel he found, below ground, the same Hasmonean masonry that appeared above ground.

---

*Warren observed this slight bend with his surveying instruments. Presumably, it could be confirmed by remeasurement today. However, for political reasons, it is not feasible to undertake this exercise now.

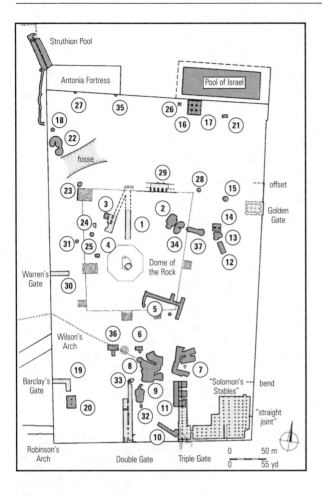

A SUBTERRANEAN LABYRINTH. In the 1860s, the complex system of structures now buried beneath the Temple Mount was extensively explored for the first and only time by Charles Warren. This plan tells us what he found. Dark blue indicates water cisterns, most of which were cut into limestone bedrock, and light blue shows underground passageways.

Herodian remains in "Solomon's Stables" (lower right) indicate that this space was used as underground storerooms during the Herodian period. These structures were rebuilt in their present form probably during the early Islamic period, when the Dome of the Rock and the El-Aqsa mosques were built. They served as stables during the Crusader period. The Pool of Israel (upper right), with a capacity of over 22 million gallons, was a large, open reservoir built as an integral part of the Herodian Temple Mount. Its purpose is unknown; the pool is not mentioned by Josephus. The Struthion Pool (upper left) is connected with the construction of the Antonia Fortress at the northwest corner of the Herodian Temple Mount, and was also an open reservoir used by the occupants of the Antonia. The quarrying of this pool may have provided the stones for the Antonia.

Warren estimated that the E-shaped cistern below the Akra (number 11, lower right) could hold 700,000 gallons of water and could have supplied the Seleucid troops with ample drinking water in case of siege. The large cistern known as the Great Sea (number 8 on the plan) is illustrated on p. 74.

Unfortunately, he stopped before reaching the limit of this Hasmonean masonry, so we don't know how far north this Hasmonean masonry continues underground. However, Warren noted that "It is probable that below the surface the first 260 [should be 240] feet of wall [from the southeast corner] are in a straight line,"[14] after which the wall changes direction slightly (to the northeast). This slight change in direction, I believe, reflects a change in masonry deep below ground.

The point at which this masonry would change, according to my speculation, based on the bend Warren observed, is exactly 861 feet, or 500 royal cubits, south of the projected northeast corner of the square pre-Herodian Temple Mount. The southeastern corner of the pre-Herodian Temple Mount is probably still in existence deep below the ground.

The southern wall of this square pre-Herodian Temple Mount should be located parallel to the northern wall, beginning at the southeast corner we have just located. The southern wall should intersect with the continuation of the step/wall, the only pre-Herodian archaeological

MAP IN HAND AND SPADE AT THE READY, Charles Warren (below left) prepares to explore a rock-cut conduit under what we now call Robinson's Arch, at the southwestern corner of the Herodian Temple Mount. Warren's often heroic research has provided us with most of our knowledge about what is under the Temple Mount. Sergeant Henry Birtles (right), Warren's assistant, a solitary candle illuminating his way, climbs a rope ladder amid huge fallen blocks below and behind Robinson's Arch, actually the beginning of an arch that springs from the western wall of the Temple Mount near the southwest corner. The "arch" was long thought to have originally supported a bridge connecting the Temple Mount and the upper city across the valley to the west. More recently—based on excavations directed by Benjamin Mazar since 1967—it has been identified by architect Brian Lalor as the support for a wide staircase leading down into the valley. These drawings, from 1870-1871, are by William "Crimea" Simpson, dispatched by the Illustrated London News to record Warren's exploits.

remains visible on the Temple Mount. (The masonry near the Golden Gate is also a visible remnant of the pre-Herodian Temple Mount. But the step is on the Temple Mount, while the masonry near the Golden Gate is in the outer wall of the Temple Mount.)

If our hypothesis is correct, then the description of the Temple Mount in *Middot* does indeed relate to the Temple Mount as it was repaired after the return from Babylon. No doubt the returning exiles, largely impoverished, did little more than repair the existing structure; they surely did not create new walls and fortifications. Accordingly, this square Temple Mount was probably the same as that which existed before the Babylonian destruction of Jerusalem in 586 B.C.—the Temple Mount of the First Temple period.

The Bible does not describe Solomon's Temple Mount, although a Solomonic Great Court round about the Temple and the Royal Palace is mentioned in 1 Kings 7:2. A *temenos*, or sacred enclosure, excavated by Professor Avraham Biran at Tel Dan, although much smaller, is also nearly square.* The *temenos* at Dan was probably built by Jeroboam I in the tenth century, shortly after Solomon's death (1 Kings 12:28-31). Is it possible that this square *temenos* was modeled on Solomon's Jerusalem Temple Mount?

Perhaps more relevant is the visionary temple described in Ezekiel 40-43. Adding up the dimensions of the gates and the two courts, as described in Ezekiel 40, this temple area also forms a square—of exactly 500 cubits to a side!

Several elements in our plan of the pre-Herodian Temple Mount are admittedly conjectural, but they tend to be confirmed by additional details.

One such detail involves the villain of the Jewish holiday of Hanukkah and a cistern investigated by Warren. Hanukkah celebrates the Maccabean victory (in 167 B.C.) over Antiochus IV Epiphanes, which returned Jerusalem to Jewish sovereignty for the first time since the Babylonian destruction of 586 B.C. The Seleucid monarch who had ruled Palestine was thereafter (in 142 B.C.) replaced with a dynasty of Jewish rulers known as Hasmoneans. The 25-year-long Maccabean revolt finally freed

*John C. Laughlin, "The Remarkable Discoveries at Tel Dan," **BAR**, September/October 1981.

HUGE, FINGERLIKE OPENINGS cut their way through the massive underground water cistern known as the Great Sea (number 8 on the plan on p. 71). Painted by William "Crimea" Simpson, this scene conveys a sense of the Temple Mount's underground installations—now inaccessible due to Muslim religious and political sensitivities. Cut 43 feet below the level of the Temple Mount, this cistern was entered by a staircase from beneath the site of the former Akra fortress. Ritmeyer suggests that stones cut from this cistern may have supplied the material for the Hasmonean extension of the Temple Mount platform.

the Jews from foreign rule. Before his ouster the Seleucid ruler Antiochus had built a fortress called the Akra for his garrison from which the Jewish population could be controlled. After the successful Jewish revolt, Simon Maccabee razed the Akra and, according to Josephus, also leveled "the very mountain itself upon which the Akra happened to stand, that so the Temple might be higher than it."[15]

The location of the Akra has been hotly debated by scholars.[16] Josephus provides two clues: It stood "in the Lower City,"[17] and "adjoined to and overlooked the Temple."[18] The Lower City is always understood as referring to the southeastern hill of Jerusalem, directly south of the Temple Mount, and also known as the City of David. One would therefore expect to find the Akra south of the Temple Mount, and, if adjoined to the Temple, as Josephus says, directly adjacent to the pre-Herodian Temple Mount. South of the Temple Mount, the hill slopes away rapidly in all directions. If the Akra overlooked the Temple, this would be another reason to place it very near the southern wall of the pre-Herodian Temple Mount.[19]

As Professor Mazar has pointed out, there is a relatively flat area, perhaps the result of Simon Maccabee's work, at the center of the southern wall of the pre-Herodian Temple Mount. And that is where I would locate the Akra.

The average level of the bedrock here is 2,400 feet, while the Temple Mount courts, directly to the north, are only 20 feet higher, so that it is not difficult to imagine a fortress here that was high enough to overlook the Temple.

This brings us to one of the most unusual cisterns under the Temple Mount. It is a curiously shaped cistern, like a letter E, unlike all the other cisterns under the Temple Mount, which are mainly irregular in shape. According to Warren, this E-shaped cistern could hold 700,000 gallons

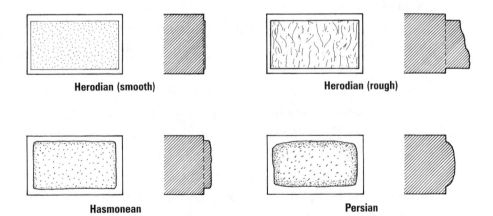

Herodian (smooth)   **Herodian (rough)**

Hasmonean   **Persian**

KEEP AN EYE ON THE BOSS. To the untrained eye, building blocks from various periods resemble one another. But the raised central area (the boss), surrounded by a margin, is the tip-off to the date of the block. Shown here in head-on and side views is masonry from the Herodian period with a low, flat, smooth boss (top left); Herodian masonry with an unfinished boss, used below the intended ground level (top right); Hasmonean masonry with a rough, projecting boss (bottom left); and Persian masonry with a rounded, bulging boss (bottom right).

of water. It sits directly under the area where we have placed the Akra. Apparently it was especially cut to provide Antiochus' garrisons with an ample supply of water in case of siege.

Shortly after I suggested this possibility to Mazar, he had a visit from Professor J. Schwartz of Bar-Ilan University, who was looking for the location of some cisterns on the Temple Mount mentioned in another tractate of the Mishnah, *Eruvin*. One of these cisterns was called "the cistern of the Akra." Here was Professor Schwartz who had a name without a cistern, while we had a cistern without a name! Putting the two together, we realized that we had additional evidence for locating the Akra adjacent to the southern wall of the pre-Herodian Temple Mount.

This conclusion was further supported by Warren's observation concerning the foundations of a massive wall in this cistern, apparently designed to support massive construction above.

Josephus also tells us that there was a direct entrance from the Akra to the Temple Mount, another reason to locate it where we have.*

If the E-shaped cistern is the cistern of the Akra as mentioned in the Mishnah, the fact that its northern edge is adjacent to the proposed southern line of the square Temple Mount tends to confirm our placement of that line.

Further confirmation that the square Temple Mount was where we have located it comes from the position of some of the other underground cisterns: Several similar small round cisterns appear along the northern, western and southern walls of this square Temple Mount.

Along the northern line near the eastern wall is cistern 15, on the inner edge of the platform. It would conveniently catch the rainwater runoff from the Temple Mount.

Cisterns 23 and 28 are located just outside the northern wall of the platform. They were probably located *inside* towers built along the northern wall to defend against an attack from that direction.

On the western line, cistern 31 has a location very similar to that of cistern 15 on the north, and probably fulfilled a similar function. The same goes for cistern 33 on the southern wall.

---

*This direct entrance was probably the forerunner of the Triple Gate in the southern wall of the present Temple Mount.

The next set of details leads to a completely new discovery: a Hasmonean addition to the First Temple-period square Temple Mount. That Herod enlarged the Temple Mount is well known, both from literary sources and archaeological evidence. The "straight joint," or seam, in the eastern wall marks the point at which Herod began his addition; south of this "straight joint" is clearly Herodian masonry.

But only now have we been able to identify a Hasmonean addition to the original square Temple Mount. We have frequently referred in this chapter to the pre-Herodian Temple Mount. But in fact there were two pre-Herodian Temple Mounts: (1) the original Temple Mount of the First Temple period (rebuilt by those returning from the Babylonian Exile) and (2) the Temple Mount as enlarged in the Hasmonean period in 141 B.C. by an addition on the south. It was this latter Temple Mount that Herod the Great (37-4 B.C.) enlarged.

Once we have demonstrated this, we may speak of the original square pre-Hasmonean Temple Mount, the enlarged Hasmonean Temple Mount and the further enlarged Herodian Temple Mount.

As previously noted, the Maccabean revolt of 167 B.C. successfully expelled the Seleucid ruler Antiochus IV Epiphanes and instituted the Jewish Hasmonean dynasty. The hated Akra—the Seleucid tower south of the square Temple Mount that rose higher than the Temple and from which Antiochus could control the Jewish masses, most of whom (since the return from the Babylonian Exile) lived in the Lower City, south of this tower—was destroyed. In 141 B.C. Simon Maccabee starved out the last remaining Seleucid garrison and then razed the Akra. According to 1 Maccabees 13:52, Simon Maccabee "strengthened the fortifications of the Temple Mount by the side of the Akra, and took up residence there with his men." This seems to indicate that the area once occupied by the Akra was incorporated into the Temple Mount. Archaeology can now confirm this.

The Hasmonean masonry north of the "straight joint" appears to have been part of their enlargement of the square Temple Mount, in the area where the Akra had stood. The Hasmonean stones have been laid in a "header and stretcher"* fashion, indicating a corner construction.

Text continues on page 83

THE SOUTHERN END OF THE EASTERN WALL. The drawings and photos highlight features from two different building periods: second-century B.C. Hasmonean and first-century B.C. Herodian. Southernmost (photo opposite, left, and drawing below) are the remains of a Herodian tower, demarcated by a slightly deepening projection of the building blocks as they go up. The drawing shows the tower reconstructed as it probably was. Three windows, now filled in, once opened from about midway up the tower. To the right of the tower and slightly below its windows were two entrances that led to storage vaults beneath the Temple platform. Now filled in, the entrances have the appearance on the drawing of a pair of windows. The Herodian southern extension of the eastern wall began just to the right of these passageways. The point where the Herodian extension began is easily visible today as a seam in the masonry wall, usually called the "straight joint" (photo opposite, right), created by the addition of the Herodian extension. On the left (southern) side of the straight joint are smooth-bossed Herodian blocks; on the right are rough-bossed Hasmonean blocks.

The bend in the wall that indicates the beginning of the Hasmonean extension is very slight. It can only be observed atop the wall, looking north from the southeast corner. The bend is therefore not detectable in the photo opposite, bottom. However, the bend begins where a column, called the Column of Mohammed and dating probably from the early Islamic period, protrudes from the wall (at right in the photo). In the drawing at left, a dotted line shows where the wall would be if it did not "bend"; the difference is small, but clear. If the wall line from the southeast corner to the "bend" is projected north for 650 feet, the resulting wall—at the northern end of these 650 feet—would be 8 feet west of the actual eastern wall.

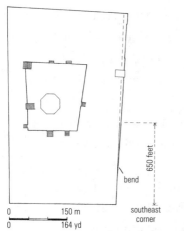

0   150 m
0   164 yd

bend

650 feet

southeast corner

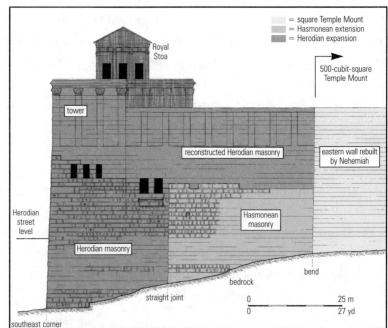

= square Temple Mount
= Hasmonean extension
= Herodian expansion

Royal Stoa

500-cubit-square Temple Mount

tower

reconstructed Herodian masonry

eastern wall rebuilt by Nehemiah

Herodian street level

Hasmonean masonry

Herodian masonry

bend

bedrock

straight joint

0   25 m
0   27 yd

southeast corner

"straight joint"

GARO NALBANDIAN

THE NORTHERN PART OF THE EASTERN WALL.

The drawing at right shows this portion of the wall as it appears today (top) and as it may have appeared before and after the Herodian addition (bottom). (The Herodian addition begins at the offset and extends to the right.) The Golden Gate (below) may have been built over the original Temple Mount's Eastern Gate. Ritmeyer identifies two monoliths (large, upright stone blocks), visible only from inside the Golden Gate, as the jambs for the Eastern Gate. These monoliths are about 12 and 15 feet high. Ritmeyer also identifies the lowest course visible above ground on either side of the outside of the Golden Gate as sixth-century B.C. masonry from the time of Nehemiah, characterized by large, bulging bosses. The photo opposite, left, and the drawing below show a closeup of this course from the north looking toward the Golden Gate. The courses above this date to a later period. Note that this lowest course ends at the bottom right of the photo and drawing. This is the offset. North of the offset (to the right) is Herodian masonry, marking the point where the northern Herodian extension begins. In the photo opposite, right, and the drawing opposite, bottom, we see this same offset at lower left, with a course of Herodian masonry extending immediately to the right of it.

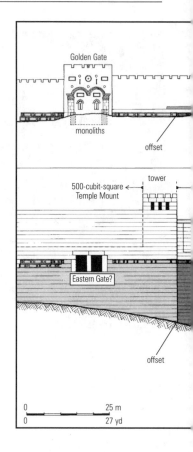

GARO NALBANDIAN

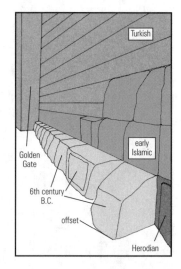

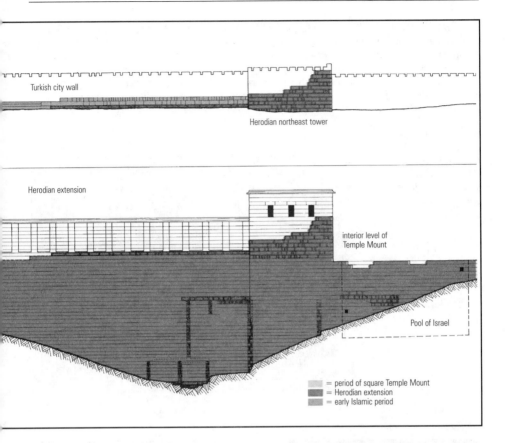

Turkish city wall

Herodian northeast tower

Herodian extension

interior level of
Temple Mount

Pool of Israel

= period of square Temple Mount
= Herodian extension
= early Islamic period

GARO NALBANDIAN

GARO NALBANDIAN

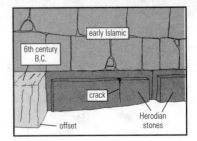

early Islamic

6th century
B.C.

crack

offset

Herodian
stones

A HERODIAN TOWER ON THE NORTHEASTERN EXTENSION. Jutting forward from the eastern wall, this tower (bottom) guarded the northeastern extension of Herod's Temple Mount. A Muslim funerary plaque (at left in photo below) now stands above the unfinished boss of a Herodian building block; this block is the northernmost element of a Herodian course along the eastern wall and adjoins (that is, it is bonded to) the northeastern tower. Note that the bottom course of the wall is aligned with the bottom course of the tower, indicating that they were built at the same time. This evidence clearly identifies the protruding tower as originally Herodian. The two higher courses of the eastern wall shown here do not line up with courses on the tower and are later. Author Ritmeyer dates these higher courses to the Islamic period.

There is no doubt that this masonry is earlier than the Herodian masonry south of it. We know this not only because of the obvious corner construction and the two different types of masonry on either side of the "straight joint," but, in addition, a careful examination of the Hasmonean stones north of the "straight joint" shows that parts of their southern margins were cut away at several places to create a better key to fit into the Herodian stones south of the "straight joint."

This Hasmonean masonry extends underground I believe, for 132 feet north of the "straight joint" to the previously mentioned bend in the eastern wall, that is, to the southeast corner of the original, square Temple Mount.

From the "straight joint," the Hasmonean wall apparently turned west until it met with the extension of the west wall of the original square Temple Mount. The Hasmonean Temple Mount was most likely embellished under Hellenistic influence with porticoes all around[20] and with tunnels that gave access to the original gateways in the southern wall of the square Temple Mount—the Hulda Gates mentioned in the Mishnah.**

The E-shaped cistern, previously mentioned, helps confirm this Hasmonean extension to the square Temple Mount. Just northwest of the E-shaped cistern, the cistern of the Akra, is the largest of the cisterns under the Temple Mount, Warren's cistern 8, known as the "Great Sea." Unfortunately, the cisterns under the Temple Mount are inaccessible today because of Muslim religious and political sensitivities. Accordingly, we have to be content with a fairly one-dimensional view of them. However, on a visit to the London office of the Palestine Exploration Fund, I saw not only the original records of Warren, Wilson, Conder, etc., but also a painting of the "Great Sea" by William Simpson, who had been sent out to Jerusalem as illustrator for the *Illustrated London News*. (He was known as "Crimea" Simpson because of his experiences in the Crimean War). This painting is published here (on p. 74).[21]

Apart from adding to our "feel" for the underground cisterns, now tan-

---

*Stretchers are laid lengthwise in the wall, the long side facing out. Headers are laid with the short side facing out. In "header and stretcher" construction, headers and stretchers alternate. This gives a wall much greater strength, especially where needed at corners.

**The Double and Triple Gates on the southern wall of the Herodian Temple Mount that can still be identified are frequently, but incorrectly, referred to as the Hulda Gates. The Hulda Gates mentioned in *Middot* 2:1 were located in the southern wall of the original square Temple Mount.

talizingly inaccessible, careful study of the painting and a comparison with the plans of the underground cisterns led to a valuable confirmation of the Hasmonean extension.

Simpson's painting shows a view to the north inside the gigantic cistern. The entrance was from the south, reached by a narrow staircase that begins just outside (south) of the square Temple Mount. The entrance was apparently dug on the site of the destroyed Akra. The cavern seems to be mostly rock-cut with columns left in place for support; its curious shape indicates that it may have incorporated earlier cisterns or caverns. The plans also show it to have several shafts to the surface, two of which are visible in the painting. Warren records the depth of the cistern as 43 feet. Apart from the entrance, the cistern was protected under the original Temple Mount.

If the "Great Sea" cistern had been in existence at the time of the building of the Akra, it would have been unnecessary to build the E-shaped cistern (cistern 11), which, as we have seen, was cut especially to supply the Seleucid garrison with water. It therefore follows that the "Great Sea" cistern was built after the destruction of the Akra and the subsequent Hasmonean extension of the Temple Mount to the south. (The cutting of this cistern may have supplied the stones for the Hasmonean extension.) This cistern may be one of the three described in Mishnah *Eruvin* 10:14:

> They [the Priests] may draw water with a wheel on the
> Sabbath from the Golah-cistern and from the Great Cistern,
> and from the Cistern of the Akra on a Festival-day.

We have already identified the Cistern of the Akra with cistern 11 and we have reason to suggest that cistern 5 can be identified with the Golah-cistern. The cistern pictured in Simpson's painting is, therefore, probably the one described in *Eruvin* as the "Great Cistern."

Our location of the square Temple Mount and the Hasmonean extension illuminates the way in which Herod the Great extended the Temple Mount as it stood at the beginning of his reign. Herod's extension also tends to confirm the location of the square Temple Mount.

The northern wall of Herod's Temple Mount was completely destroyed by the Romans in 70 A.D. when they conquered Jerusalem, burned the Temple and effectively ended the First Jewish Revolt (although the Masada rebels held out for three more years). However, the northeast corner has been preserved and, together with the rocky foundations of the Antonia Fortress at the northwest corner,[22] enables us to draw the northern wall's line.

Herod's northern addition to the Temple Mount explains a strange notice in *Middot* 1:3 that "the Tadi Gate [on the north] has no purpose at all." This was probably because the Tadi Gate was the northern gate of the original square Temple Mount. When Herod buried this area with fill to create his northern court, the Tadi Gate was completely buried and thus rendered useless.[23]

At the northwest corner of his enlarged Temple Mount, on a rock scarp, Herod built the Antonia Fortress. Its location, first suggested by Father Pierre Benoit,[24] has been widely accepted.

The western wall of Herod's extension still exists for the full length (as does the southern wall), so it is a simple matter to extend the northern wall to the point where it would meet the western wall.

From Herod's western wall, the Temple Mount could be ascended through two lower gates, now called Warren's Gate and Barclay's Gate, after the scholars who discovered and identified them. (Two upper gates were built over Wilson's Arch and Robinson's Arch.)

In chapter 1, my wife, Kathleen, and I discussed the external problems relating to Barclay's Gate. The internal problems are just as fascinating. From Barclay's Gate, a subterranean internal stairway led up to the surface of the Temple Mount, opening on the western Temple court (see plans on p. 68). Similar underground passageways led up to the Temple Mount from the Double and Triple gates on the southern wall, but these passageways are straight. The underground stairway from Barclay's Gate is L-shaped. Starting at the gate, the passageway proceeds in an easterly direction for 84 feet inside the wall. Here, in Warren's cistern 19, Warren describes a flat dome over the passageway at this point. The passageway then turns south; its continuation is found in Warren's cistern 20, from which the surface of the Temple Mount was probably reached.

The eastern wall of the passageway at the point where it turns south

De Vogüé 1864

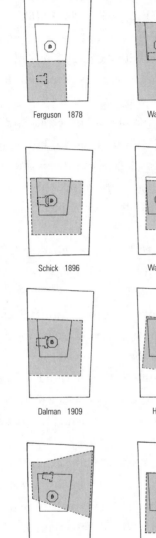

Ferguson 1878

Warren 1880

Conder 1884

Schick 1896

Watson 1896

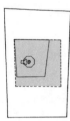

Mommert 1903

Dalman 1909

Hollis 1934

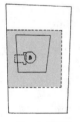

Vincent 1954

Kaufman 1983

Ritmeyer 1985

LIKE A MOVING TARGET, past researchers have shifted the precise location of the original Temple Mount. Shown here are a dozen theories, culminating in author Leen Ritmeyer's proposal. Shown in black are the Temple Mount and the Muslim Platform within it as they appear today; the octagonal shape is the Dome of the Rock with the es-Sakhra rock, the highest point of the mount, at its center. The dashed lines represent the location of the original Temple Mount platform from the time of the First Temple as put forth by the various theorists; the dashed T-shape indicates where within the platform they placed the Temple itself. Ritmeyer, noting that the Mishnah says the Temple Mount's largest open space "was at the south, second largest, at the east, third largest, at the north, and least, at the west" locates the Temple atop es-Sakhra, where the Dome of the Rock is today. (For citations to various theorists, see endnote 28 on p. 114.)

under the flat dome has a distinct batter; that is, each higher course of stones in the eastern wall of cistern 19 is set in slightly from the one below.[25] (Incidentally, the Herodian Temple Mount wall also has a batter.) The wall with a batter in cistern 19 appears to be the western wall of the Hasmonean Temple Mount built after the square platform was extended to the south in the wake of the destruction of the Akra.

The reason then for the L-shape of the underground stairway leading up from Barclay's Gate is that Herod's builders built the southern part of this stairway alongside the existing (Hasmonean) western wall, instead of attempting to cut through the wall, which would have been very difficult. Here again we find confirmation of the location of the square Temple Mount and its Hasmonean extension.

The other gate from Herod's western Temple Mount wall up to the Temple Mount is Warren's Gate, north of Barclay's Gate. When Warren examined this gate, he described it as cistern 30, but he correctly identified it as having been a gateway tunnel before it was used as a cistern. It is 18 feet wide, the same as the passageway from Barclay's Gate. The passageway in Warren's Gate has a vaulted roof. I believe that this is the first part of another L-shaped subterranean stairway up to the Temple Mount. Today, the passage ends approximately 18 feet before the projected western wall of the original square Temple Mount. I believe the final 18 feet of the passageway was filled in at a later date, as was the continuation of the L along the original Temple Mount wall that led up to the western court of Herod's addition.

It is interesting that even on the southern wall, the underground passageways from Herod's Double and Triple gates are approximately 240 feet long, opening on the Temple Mount almost precisely on the southern line of the original square Temple Mount, providing additional confirmation of our location.

Now, having located the original Temple Mount platform (as well as the Hasmonean and Herodian additions), we turn to the final question: Where, on the original Temple Mount, was the Temple located?

My research into the exact location of the Temple building is not yet complete. Many factors must be taken into consideration, but enough information has already been gathered to draw a preliminary plan.

It is generally agreed that Herod's Temple stood at the same place as the Temple built by Solomon, which, obviously, stood within the original square Temple Mount. The square Temple Mount actually formed the great court surrounding the Temple.

One might expect the Temple to be located in the center of the square Temple Mount (in Ezekiel's visionary temple the altar is in the center; in the Temple Scroll the entrance to the Temple itself is located in the center). But here, that is not so. Es-Sakhra, the rock formation over which the Dome of the Rock is built, lies to the northwest of the center of the square Temple Mount. This mass of natural rock is the top of the middle part of the eastern hill of Jerusalem, and Josephus tells us that the Temple was built on the top of the mountain—that is, on top of es-Sakhra.[26]

If es-Sakhra was the location of the Temple, then the courts surrounding the Temple would all have different dimensions. That is precisely what *Middot* 2:1 tells us: "The Temple Mount was five hundred cubits by five hundred. Its largest [open space] was at the south, second largest, at the east, third largest, at the north, and least, at the west."

The spaces referred to in this text are undoubtedly the different parts of the outer court that surrounded the inner court of the Temple (excluding, apparently, the Court of the Women).

Taking these guidelines into consideration, I drew the Temple according to scale, using the specific measurements given in *Middot*, and, while experimenting with the dimensions referred to above, hit upon an interesting picture: In order to fulfill the requirements of *Middot* for the southern court to have been the largest, and with the dimensions of the other parts of the outer court diminishing as one proceeds in a counterclockwise direction, the Temple must have been built around es-Sakhra.

Despite some proposals that would place the Temple north of es-Sakhra,[27] I have become convinced that the Temple was built over es-Sakhra, where researchers of the last century and a half have instinctively placed it.[28] The difference between the approach of most previous researchers and my approach is that they used es-Sakhra as a starting point, while I reached this location after first having located the square Temple Mount, and working, so to speak, from the outside toward the center.

Another factor supporting my conclusion is the fact that, according to *Middot*, the Temple had foundations 6 cubits high. But why would this be necessary if the Temple were built on bedrock?

Es-Sakhra now stands about 5 to 6 feet above the floor of the Dome of the Rock. A short distance outside the Dome of the Rock (in cisterns 1, 3 and 5) Warren found the difference in height from the top of es-Sakhra to bedrock to be 13 to 15 feet. Taking into consideration that the bedrock would gently slope up from the points Warren measured to the base of es-Sakhra, it seems that es-Sakhra stands about 10 feet above the bedrock immediately surrounding it. Ten feet equals 6 cubits, the height of the Temple foundation specified in *Middot*. It stands to reason that these foundations—6 cubits high—were necessary to "bury" es-Sakhra in order to create a level platform on which the Temple could be built.[29]

With this positioning of the Temple on the square Temple Mount, for the first time, all the factors—topographical, archaeological and historical—have been taken into account. And all seem to fit precisely.

While I believe that there is already enough evidence to place the Temple firmly over the top of es-Sakhra, I intend to undertake further study of the historical sources in light of the topography and architecture of the Temple Mount which will, hopefully, enable me to refine this proposal still further.

Much of the research for this article was supported by a grant from the Biblical Archaeology Society through the generosity of Joseph G. Hurley, Esq., and his wife Davia Solomon, Esq.

BAR editor Hershel Shanks was one of the first people to recognize the importance of this research and I am indebted to him for his interest and support. His searching questions during the editorial process have been most helpful in making this chapter clear and understandable to the lay reader.

I would like to acknowledge the continual support of my wife, Kathleen, whom I first met on the Temple Mount excavations, and her many contributions to this chapter.

I am indebted to the late Professor Nahman Avigad, director of the archaeological excavations in the Jewish Quarter of the Old City of Jerusalem, by whom I was employed at the time of the early stages of the research, for having given me the opportunity to dedicate myself to a study with Professor Benjamin Mazar.

The valuable comments and suggestions made by Jerome Murphy-O'Connor, O.P., professor of New Testament at the École Biblique et Archéologique Française in Jerusalem, during the later stages of the research were much appreciated.

I am also very grateful to Dr. John P. Kane of the Faculty of Theology at the University of Manchester, U.K, for his guidance during my Ph.D research. His wide-ranging knowledge of the archaeology of Jerusalem has been of great help to me. I especially appreciate the use of his extensive library, which he unselfishly put at my disposal.

The kind donation by Edgar and Marjorie Hall of Nottingham, U.K., of a complete set of Warren's Plans, Elevations, Sections, etc. was, needless to say, a valuable asset to the research.

6

THE ARK OF THE COVENANT
WHERE IT STOOD IN SOLOMON'S TEMPLE

Leen Ritmeyer

In the previous chapter I identified the location of the original 500-cubit-square Temple Mount. By now, this location is well established in the archaeological world, having been adopted, for example, in the latest edition of the archaeological encyclopedia of the Holy Land published by the Israel Exploration Society.[1]

My goal was always more than this, however. I was convinced that it was possible, on the basis of these findings, to locate the site of the Temple itself. The method of working from the outside in, in relation to the Temple Mount, had been sanctioned by the success of its discovery. Having narrowed down the search to this square, it would be logical to trace the location of the actual Temple from the archaeological remains found in this reduced area. Close familiarity with the Biblical and extra-Biblical sources on the Temple, gained from years of prior research into the Temple Mount, would ensure that the emerging picture could be tested against the reality of history.

At the end of the previous chapter, I briefly discussed the location of the

Temple. Based on then-preliminary considerations, I placed it, not in the center of the original Temple Mount, but over the rock mass lying beneath the Dome of the Rock, generally referred to as es-Sakhra, "the Rock" in Arabic. But, as I wrote then, I intended to refine my proposal still further. This chapter is the fulfillment of that promise.

Moreover, as the research gathered its own momentum, other questions that I had not even considered could be answered were unexpectedly resolved. I now believe that, without having gone in search of it, the research has directed us to the very spot where the Ark of the Covenant stood within the Holy of Holies.

My reasons for placing the Temple over es-Sakhra are briefly as follows: Few would contest that Herod's Temple stood on the same site as that of Solomon. Herod's Jewish subjects barely allowed him to rebuild the Second Temple—a change of site would have been inconceivable. The first-century A.D. Jewish historian, Josephus, tells us that Herod's Temple was built at the top of the mountain.[2] It is clear to anyone who visits the site or who examines a photograph of the area that the Dome of the Rock enshrines the rocky summit of the mount.

Placed here, with the Holy of Holies over es-Sakhra, the courtyards on the four sides of the Temple conform to their relative sizes as specified in *Middot*, a tractate of the Mishnah (the earliest rabbinic codification of the law, from about 200 A.D.). According to *Middot* 2.1, "The Temple Mount was 500 cubits by 500 cubits. Its largest [open space, i.e., courtyard] at the south, second largest, at the east, third largest, at the north and least, at the west." These requirements can be satisfied only if the Holy of Holies of the Temple is placed over es-Sakhra.*

Middot 4.6 also tells us that the foundation of the Temple was 6 cubits, or about 10 feet, high. That is an unusually high foundation. Es-Sakhra now stands almost 6 feet above the floor of the Dome of the Rock. If we take into consideration that the bedrock is located another 3 feet, 3 inches

---

*Some proposals have put the altar on es-Sakhra, but then es-Sakhra would have disappeared completely below it, as es-Sakhra is smaller than the altar. According to *Middot* 3.1, the altar was 32 cubits (55 feet, or 16.8 meters) square. Another problem with placing the altar over es-Sakhra is that the well-known cave that lies below es-Sakhra, which was supposed to have drained off the blood to the Kidron Valley, would be in the wrong place, as, according to *Middot* 3.2, this original drain was located at the southwest corner of the altar, while the cave is on the southeast corner.

(1 meter) below the floor, then the rock would stand at least 9 feet above its immediate surroundings. That this is, in fact, the case is demonstrated by a re-examination of an 1873 report by the French scholar Charles Clermont-Ganneau. Clermont-Ganneau tells us that he witnessed a small excavation near the eastern door of the Dome of the Rock in which he saw *terra rossa*, the typical red earth found immediately above bedrock, at a depth of 2 feet (57 centimeters) below the paving in this area. The excavation continued to a depth of 3 feet (90 centimeters), but bedrock was still not encountered, although the feeling was that it could not

THE DOME AND THE ROCK. One of the most spectacular buildings in the world, the Dome of the Rock has dominated the skyline of the Old City of Jerusalem since its construction by Caliph Abd al-Malik in 691 A.D.; so identified with the city is the dome that it frequently serves as an icon for Jerusalem.

Directly below the 108-foot-high dome lies es-Sakhra, the rock mass from which, according to Muslim tradition, Mohammed ascended to heaven on his night journey to Jerusalem. Jewish tradition views the rock as the place where Abraham nearly sacrificed Isaac (Muslims counter that it was Abraham's other son, their ancestor Ishmael, instead). Everyone agrees, however, that Jerusalem's First Temple, built by Solomon, and the Second Temple, greatly expanded by King Herod, stood somewhere on the same mount that now holds the Dome of the Rock, though opinions differ over precisely where. Author Leen Ritmeyer, in the previous chapter, described the location of the original square Temple Mount; while engaged in his own night flight to Jerusalem (carried aloft by an airplane), Ritmeyer pinpointed what he believes is the very spot where the Ark of the Covenant rested within the Temple, as he details in this chapter.

have been far away.[3] Furthermore, in 1959 Italian Franciscan scholar Bellarmino Bagatti noticed bedrock at several places below the floor during extensive repair operations conducted at that time. According to his observations, the general appearance of "the Rock" was that it was level but dipped down towards the outer walls of the Dome of the Rock. As the

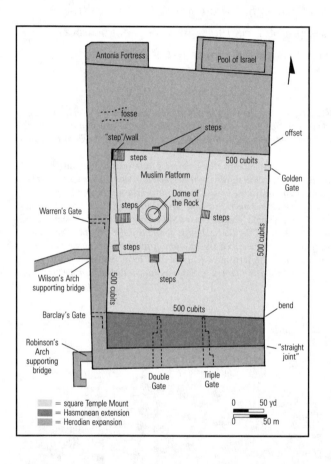

WHERE WAS THE TEMPLE? *This plan shows the Temple Mount as expanded by Herod to hold his lavishly rebuilt Second Temple. The main area in the middle is the square Temple Mount that supported the First Temple. In the previous chapter, Ritmeyer established the location of the square Temple Mount, thanks to a telltale "step" on the northwest corner of the present-day Muslim Platform. Ritmeyer noticed that the stairway was parallel to the eastern wall of the Temple Mount and not, like the seven other stairways, to the Muslim Platform. He further noticed that the bottom step of this stairway was not really a step but a line of pre-Herodian stones, leading him to wonder whether it was actually part of an early wall. His hunch was confirmed when he discovered that the distance from this bottom "step" to the eastern wall was 500 royal cubits—the distance given in the Mishnah (an early compendium of rabbinic law) for the sides of the square Temple Mount. From this newly ascertained northeast corner, it is another 500 cubits to a bend in the eastern wall, which marks the beginning of a southern addition to the square Temple Mount.*

Two criteria allowed Ritmeyer then to determine that the Temple had stood on the area now occupied by the Dome of the Rock. First, the location is the highest point on the mount and, second, it matches a description given by the Mishnah for the Temple: The largest open space on the Temple Mount, according to the Mishnah, was on the south, the second on the east, the third on the north and the least on the west. Having identified the square Temple Mount and the location of the Temple, Ritmeyer was left with one last challenge: Could he pinpoint the Holy of Holies—and perhaps the spot where the Ark of the Covenant stood?

outer face of the walls of the Temple were located 25 cubits (41 feet) away from the foot of es-Sakhra (*Middot* 4.7), we can therefore safely add at least another foot to the 9 feet just mentioned, bringing the total difference in height between the top of es-Sakhra and the outer walls of the Temple to just over 10 feet—which is exactly 6 cubits. Now we can understand why the Temple required a foundation 6 cubits high—so that the floor of the Temple would be at approximately the same level as the top of es-Sakhra, where the Ark of the Covenant could be placed in the Holy of Holies.

From the moment I identified the original Temple Mount, I knew that if I were to go further I would need to research and analyze es-Sakhra down to its minutest detail.[4] I also knew that this was going to be a formidable task, as no previous systematic archaeological research had ever been carried out on this rock mass. Israeli archaeologists, who have been eager to study every stone of the Holy Land and especially of Jerusalem, have avoided es-Sakhra like the Biblical plague sent to punish King David for taking a census (see 2 Samuel 24). Obviously the political sensitivities of the Temple Mount area are one problem. In addition, the seemingly intractable problems involved in its interpretation make it a veritable scholarly *terra incognita*, despite the fact that the site is the focus of three major world religions.

My first task was to try to make an accurate plan of es-Sakhra. I began with the measurements and description the German scholar Gustaf Dalman made in 1910.[5] Dalman's plan, in fact, proved to be highly accurate, as he was actually allowed to walk on es-Sakhra for ten minutes. In a series of subsequent visits, he made further measurements by stretching tapes over "the Rock" with the help of a mosque attendant who stood inside the fence. Based on my own observations and photographs taken from the ambulatory, high above, under the dome, I then added new features. As far as measurements are concerned, I have found that pacing out the dimensions of a structure can be very accurate. It is a method I have used for a long time when circumstances do not allow for a full survey. My normal step for measuring is 95 centimeters, or 3 feet, 1 inch.

The next task was to try, based on this plan, to reconstruct es-Sakhra as it had existed in the First Temple period. Such an exercise, of course, requires an understanding of the Temple's history—indeed, Jerusalem's history—through the ages. The original appearance of es-Sakhra can be deduced only by eliminating all the changes made to it since it was housed in Solomon's Temple.

Through all the vicissitudes of the site during the time of the First and Second temples, it appears from the sources that whenever the Temple was despoiled or damaged it was always built up again. So it was that the damage inflicted on it by the immediate predecessors of King Joash was followed by his extensive repairs under the guidance of Jehoiada the high priest (2 Kings 12:1-16; 2 Chronicles 24:1-14). Later, the earthquake damage that affected the Temple in the last year of King Uzziah was partially repaired by King Jotham (2 Kings 15:35; 2 Chronicles 27:3). Again, the sanctuary was cleansed by King Hezekiah (2 Chronicles 29:3-19) after the replacement of the scripturally prescribed altar by one brought in from Damascus by King Ahaz. Following on the perilous times of the reign of Manasseh and his son Amon, when the Ark of the Covenant was apparently removed by the priests for safekeeping, their successor Josiah had the ark restored to the Holy of Holies (2 Chronicles 35:3). The Babylonian destruction of the Temple in 586 B.C. was followed by its reconstruction by Ezra, Jeshua, Zerubbabel and Nehemiah after a 70-year exile in Babylon. The plundering of the Temple by Antiochus Epiphanes and his sacrilegious offering of a swine on the altar was followed by

THE LUNAR-LIKE SURFACE of es-Sakhra bears the marks of 3,000 turbulent years. The plan opposite highlights some of the significant features etched into it; light blue indicates the Muslim-built piers and pillars of the Dome of the Rock, while dark blue shows Crusader alterations.

At bottom center, we can peer through a 3-foot-wide circular opening below which lies a cave known as Bir el-Arwah, the "Well of Souls." The Crusaders called it the Holy of Holies and venerated it as the site of the annunciation of John the Baptist. Medieval Christians probably lit candles here as part of their pilgrimage to the site; the hole is simply a Crusader chimney. Moving west from the hole (towards the top of the photo), we see two flat rectangular areas, each about 3 feet wide and 5 and 8 feet long, respectively. Ritmeyer recognized these areas as foundation trenches, cut to create a level surface on which foundation stones of a building could be placed. On the western edge of es-Sakhra, the Crusaders built a broad staircase. The far western edge of es-Sakhra can be seen at top, nearly abutting the balustrade; this edge is a natural rock scarp. Along the north side of es-Sakhra sits a rectangular depression measuring 4 feet, 4 inches by 2 feet, 7 inches; this extraordinary feature is examined in more detail on p. 101. Slightly further to the east we can still see signs of Crusader quarrying; in medieval times, pieces of "the Rock" were literally worth their weight in gold. Finally, in the center of es-Sakhra is a trapezoidal area that lies at the center point of the Dome of the Rock. The building was laid out from here, using a string attached to a pole to draw the circular plan of the structure.

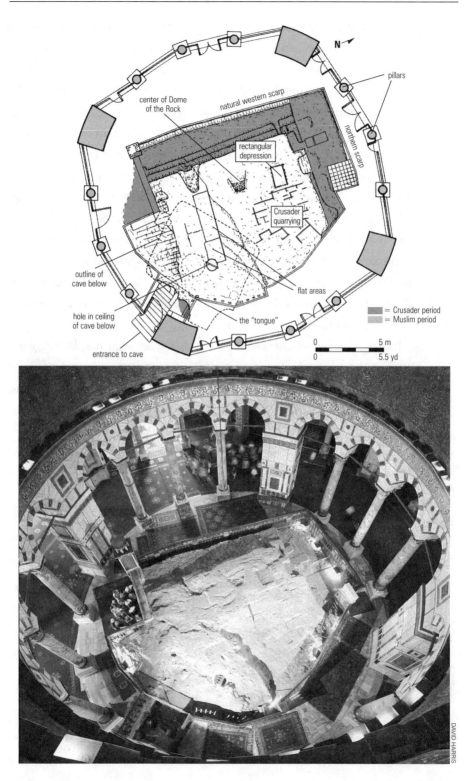

pillars

center of Dome
of the Rock

natural western scarp

rectangular
depression

northern scarp

Crusader
quarrying

outline of
cave below

flat areas

hole in ceiling
of cave below

the "tongue"

entrance to cave

= Crusader period
= Muslim period

0   5 m
0   5.5 yd

DAVID HARRIS

its rededication by the Maccabees in 164 B.C. (1 Maccabees 4:36-61; 2 Maccabees 10:1-8) and an extension of the Temple platform under the Hasmonean dynasty.

It appears that throughout this period whatever happened to the site was well documented: Damage to the Temple consisted of a breaking down of its walls or robbery of the Temple treasures. At worst, a pagan image was installed inside the Holy of Holies, as was probably the case during the reign of Manasseh (2 Kings 21:7; 2 Chronicles 33:15). The sources give us no reason to believe that there was any change in es-Sakhra or in the alignment of its foundations. Herod's rebuilding of the Temple, which commenced in 19 B.C. and which was completed approximately half a century later, afforded es-Sakhra further protection until its destruction by the Romans in 70 A.D. Herod simply took away the old foundations of the Temple and replaced them with new foundations 6 cubits high.[6]

I knew that we would have to look closely at what had befallen the Temple site during the Roman period. In the fourth decade of the second century, after the Second Jewish Revolt against Rome (132-135 A.D.), the emperor Hadrian rebuilt Jerusalem, which he renamed Aelia Capitolina,

THE FINGERS OF THE ANGEL GABRIEL, according to Muslim tradition, left their imprint on the western face of es-Sakhra. Tradition has it that the rock wanted to follow Mohammed on his ascent to heaven and had to be restrained by the angel. The north-south line of this western rock scarp is 3.5 degrees east, a very significant orientation because it parallels the western and eastern walls of the square Temple Mount (see plan, p. 94).

and made it a Roman city from which Jews were barred. Two writers of the period, Dio Cassius and Jerome, mention a temple of Jupiter built on the site of the Jewish Temple. Eyewitnesses, such as Origen and the Pilgrim of Bordeaux, mention two statues, at least one of which represented the Emperor Hadrian. Apart from this, the Temple was all but ignored during this period.

In 324 A.D. the Byzantine period began in Palestine, with the unification of the empire under Constantine. Constantine Christianized the empire. During the Byzantine period the Temple Mount was left in ruins as a sign that, as the early Christians believed, God had abandoned the Jews; the site, therefore, had no further relevance.

When Jerusalem was taken by Caliph Omar in 638 A.D., he found that es-Sakhra had been used as a dunghill, which took great Arab labor to clean.

Then, with the construction of the Dome of the Rock in the late seventh century and the reverence accorded to es-Sakhra by the Muslims, its protection was assured until the coming of the Crusaders. In 1099, the Crusaders wrested the Dome of the Rock from the Muslims and converted it into a church called Templum Domini. A cross then graced the top of the dome.

Most of the changes I detected in es-Sakhra can be attributed to the Crusader period. The history books suggest as much. According to one contemporaneous account, the reason the Crusaders mutilated es-Sakhra was, "It disfigured the Temple of the Lord."[7] When the Crusaders transformed the Dome of the Rock into a church, they cut away parts of es-Sakhra to make it more aesthetic in the eyes of westerners. They also quarried a broad staircase from the bedrock leading up to es-Sakhra on the west, so that the High Altar, which stood on top of es-Sakhra, could be reached more easily. At this time the entire rock mass was covered with marble slabs.

After Jerusalem fell to the Egyptian-Turkish Sultan Saladin (Sarah ed-Din) in the late 12th century, Muslim historians clamored in their denunciation of what the Crusaders had done to es-Sakhra. One of them described not only what the Crusaders had done, but how the Sultan had tried to undo the damage:

As for the Rock, the Franks (Crusaders) built over it a church and an altar, so that there was no longer any room for the hands that wish to seize the blessing from it or the eyes that long to see it. They had adorned it with images and statues, set up dwellings there for monks and made it into a place for the Gospel, which they venerated and exalted to the heights. Over the place of the Prophet's [Mohammed's] holy foot they set up an ornamental tabernacle with columns of marble, marking it as a place where the Messiah [Jesus] had set his foot; a holy and exalted place, where flocks of animals, among which I saw a species of pig, were carved in marble. The Rock, the object of pilgrimage, was hidden under constructions and submerged in all this sumptuous building. So that the Sultan ordered that the veil be removed, the curtain raised, the concealments taken away, the marble carried off, the stones broken, the structures demolished, the covers broken into. The Rock was to be brought to light again for visitors and revealed to observers, stripped of its covering and brought forward like a young bride. Before the conquest only a small part of the back of it was exposed, and the Unbelievers [Crusaders] had cut it about shamefully; now it appeared in all its beauty, revealed in the loveliest revelations.[8]

The Crusaders had also chipped away at es-Sakhra to raise money. These rock chips they would sell back in Europe for an equal weight of gold. As reported by an Arab historian,

The Franks had cut pieces from the Rock, some of which they carried to Constantinople and Sicily and sold, they said, for their weight in gold, making it a source of income. When the Rock reappeared to sight, the marks of these cuts were seen and men were incensed to see how it had been mutilated. Now it is on view with the wounds it suffered, preserving its honor forever, safe for Islam, within its protection and its fence.[9]

Since the time of Saladin, es-Sakhra appears to have remained untouched. Although Saladin removed the paving, the icons and other

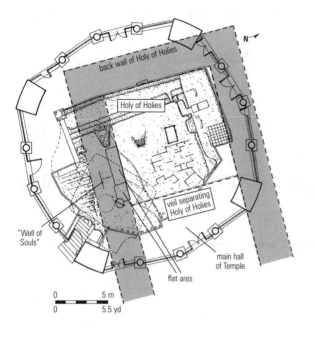

THE WALLS OF THE HOLY OF HOLIES. *Along the southern end of es-Sakhra two flat rectangular areas and other, less noticeable, flat areas to their south, just before the bedrock slopes dramatically down, combine to form a foundation trench over 10 feet wide—equal to the 6 cubit width given in the Mishnah for the thickness of the Temple walls. This yields one wall of the Temple. The back wall would have been placed against the natural rock scarp along the west, with the north wall adjacent to the northern end of es-Sakhra. Now the significance of the rectangular depression near the north end of es-Sakhra becomes clear: It sits exactly in the center of the proposed Holy of Holies.*

Crusader additions from the Dome of the Rock, he left the wrought-iron screen that stood between the columns of the inner circle of the dome. This screen remained until the restoration of 1963.

Es-Sakhra is now surrounded by a wooden balustrade and may be viewed only from outside this enclosure. This makes looking at details difficult. Es-Sakhra lies under the great golden dome, which is supported by four major piers and 12 columns, three on each side, between the piers.

As mentioned before, es-Sakhra itself stands almost 6 feet above the floor of the Dome of the Rock. The main entrance to the Dome of the Rock is on the west, so that one naturally approaches es-Sakhra from that direction. Looking at it from the west, it appears that the shape of es-Sakhra has been changed to look like a square block and fit exactly in the middle of the four major piers that support the dome. Before that happened, however, es-Sakhra must have looked almost like a circle with the pillars surrounding it.

Beneath the southeastern quadrant of es-Sakhra is a cave known as Bir el-Arwah, the "Well of Souls" (marked by a dotted line on the plan

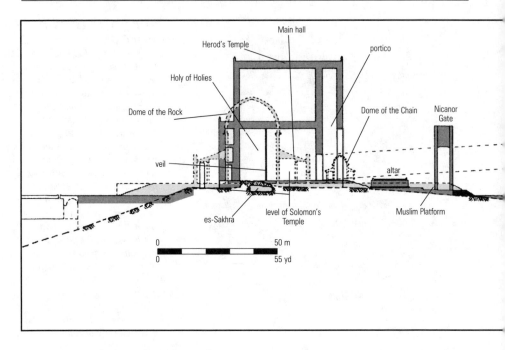

on p. 101). It has an irregular squarish shape—about 24 feet in either direction. The ceiling looks natural. The height varies from about 5 feet to almost 9 feet. Fourteen steps descend into the cave; the three lowest steps are semicircular. Two bedrock projections extend into the stairway area on either side of the steps. The one on the right as you descend is known as "the tongue." You can touch it as you descend into the cave. These projections indicate that the original width of the entrance to the cave was much narrower than it is today.

Nearly in the center of the cave's ceiling is a hole about 3 feet in diameter cutting through the bedrock to the surface of es-Sakhra. The distance from the ceiling of the cave to the surface of es-Sakhra is, at this point, 5 feet, 7 inches; there are no signs of rope marks at the edges of the top of the hole as would be the case with the wellhead of a cistern.

The hole is first mentioned in a record of a visit to the Dome of the Rock by Ali of Herat in 1173,[10] 15 years before it was taken by Saladin. As the hole is never mentioned in earlier sources, it appears very probable that it was cut by the Crusaders. We know that the Crusaders called this cave the Holy of Holies and venerated it as the site of the annunciation of John

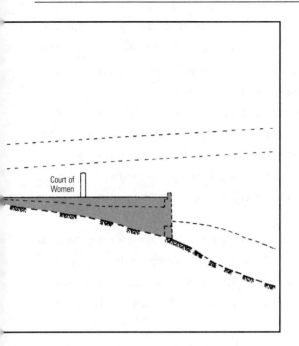

A VERTICAL SLICE. This section drawing cuts through the Temple Mount from west (left) to east (right) and shows the relative positions of Temple structures (darker shading) and the Dome of the Rock and its platform (lighter shading). Es-Sakhra is the highest point of the Temple Mount, located at the center of the Dome of the Rock and in the inner-most (and westernmost) room of the Temple, the Holy of Holies. This most sacred enclosure was walled on the south, west and north sides; a veil hung over the opening on its eastern side. The Temple's eastern orientation allowed the High Priest to look directly into the sanctuary while sprinkling the blood of the red heifer on the Mount of Olives across the Kidron Valley from the Temple.

Court of Women

the Baptist. As related in Luke 1:5-25, John's father, Zechariah, was a priest who, while officiating in the Temple, received a visitation from the angel Gabriel. Gabriel announced to him that, although both Zechariah and his wife, Elizabeth, were advanced in years, she would bear him a son. Not long thereafter Elizabeth had a son who grew up to be John the Baptist. If the cave was typical of such shrines in Crusader times, visitors would have lighted candles, so a ventilation system was imperative. The Crusaders may have cut this hole to achieve this purpose. In short, the hole in the ceiling of the cave is simply a Crusader chimney.

One of the first clues I found relating to the wall of the original Holy of Holies is on the surface of es-Sakhra adjacent to this Crusader chim-ney. Two flat, slightly depressed, rectangular areas can clearly be dis-cerned west of the hole. The smaller of the two flat areas lies to the immediate west of the hole. The other, located adjacent to the smaller one but further to the west of it, is longer. Each is about 3 feet wide; the shorter one is approximately 5 feet long and the longer about 8 feet long. The shorter one is a few inches lower than the longer one.

Gustaf Dalman had already noticed these flat areas but could not understand their purpose and did not think that the near surroundings indicated their function either.[11] He cites Rudolf Kittel, who thought that the lower one, because of its close proximity to the hole, was a receptacle for blood, channeling it into the cave below.

In countless archaeological sites I have seen rock that has been leveled to create even bases for square or rectangular foundation stones of buildings. Without cutting a foundation trench, the stones would have wobbled about, making the building unsafe. The same would be true for the walls of the Temple. In short, these flat areas were very familiar to me as foundation trenches.

But why would one of the walls of the Temple be built on es-Sakhra? Asking the right question was almost the same as providing the answer. The visible surface of es-Sakhra is approximately 43 feet by 56 feet. This is larger than the Holy of Holies in the Temple, which measured 20

COURTESY WORLD OF THE BIBLE MINISTRIES

"THE PRIESTS brought the Ark of the Covenant of YHWH to its place, in the Holy of Holies [dvir] of the Temple" (1 Kings 8:6). That "place" can now be identified as the rectangular depression in es-Sakhra that measures 2 feet, 7 inches by 4 feet, 4 inches—1.5 by 2.5 cubits—the same dimensions as the Ark of the Covenant that God commanded Moses to build in the wilderness (Exodus 25:10) and that was later housed in the Temple.

One puzzling detail: The ark, placed in this depression, would be positioned with its narrow side facing the front of the Temple. This was necessary, however, because the 10-cubit-long staves on which the ark was transported could not have been removed if the ark had been placed with its long side facing the front of the Temple: The Holy of Holies in which the ark was placed was only 20 cubits wide.

cubits—or 34 feet, 6 inches—square. If this was indeed the location of the Holy of Holies, then at least one of its walls must have been built on es-Sakhra. As es-Sakhra is also called the Foundation Stone, it would truly live up to its name if this were so.

On the southern side of the balustrade enclosing es-Sakhra additional flat areas south of the two just described can be seen, although these additional flat areas are not so well defined. Nevertheless, together with the flat areas to the west of the hole leading down to the cave, they appear to form a foundation trench for a broad wall, which would have run from east to west. The thickness of this wall, based on the measurements of this southern foundation trench, is over 10 feet (3 meters) from north to south. The bedrock to the south then slopes down steeply.

The coincidence between this measurement and the measurement given in *Middot* 4.7 for the thickness of the walls of the Second Temple— 6 cubits, or 10 feet, 4 inches—is irresistible. Preserved here on the face of es-Sakhra, despite all the Crusader insensitivity to the rock, was the imprint of the southern wall of the Holy of Holies.

Now let us look at the western face of es-Sakhra. Standing at the wooden balustrade, we find ourselves facing a natural rock scarp that rises 3 feet, 7 inches (1.09 meters) above the pavement. (The bottom of the scarp, below the floor, is difficult to see because it is so close to the balustrade.) This natural rock scarp has many deep grooves running up and down. I counted 27 grooves in the western face of the rock; in the southern part, 8 grooves are identified by the Muslims as the finger marks of the angel Gabriel, who held down es-Sakhra when it wanted to follow Mohammed during his ascent to heaven.

Although the north-south line of the rock scarp is slightly broken, the major direction is approximately 3.5 degrees east. This is a very significant number. In the previous chapter, on locating the original square Temple Mount, you will recall that the first telltale clue was a step at the base of the northwest stairway leading up to the Muslim Platform on which the Dome of the Rock is built. This step turned out to be part of a wall at the northwest corner of the original Temple Mount that was precisely parallel to the eastern wall of the Temple Mount. Both this step (hereafter "the Step") and the eastern wall of the Temple Mount are aligned almost identically to the line of the rock scarp on the western face of es-Sakhra—approximately 3.5 degrees east! The line of the rock scarp on the western face of es-Sakhra marks the inner face of the western wall of the Temple—the back wall of the Holy of Holies—perfectly parallel to the western wall of the original Temple Mount (the Step) and the eastern wall of the original Temple Mount. The back wall of the Temple stood at the foot of this natural western scarp, with es-Sakhra on the east.

The longitudinal axis of the Temple was at a right angle to this western wall. As the western scarp is natural—and therefore never changed its direction—there are no grounds to believe that the axis of the First Temple was different from that of the Second Temple.[12] Both were oriented in precisely the same west-to-east direction, with the portal on the east, facing the rising sun. Interestingly, the continuation of this axis aligns with the top of the Mount of Olives (across the Kidron Valley), where the red heifer was sacrificed (see Numbers 19). According to Middot 2.4, the high priest who burns the red heifer and stands on the top of the Mount of Olives should be able to look directly into the entrance of the sanctuary when the blood is sprinkled. This is another confirmation of my location and orientation of the Temple.*

We now have two walls of the original Holy of Holies. The distance from the wall we have identified as the southern wall of the Holy of Holies to the northern edge of es-Sakhra is 34 feet, 5 inches (10.5 meters). Converted to cubits, the result is startling: The distance is exactly 20 cubits, the Biblically prescribed measurement of each side of the Holy of Holies! Here the northern wall of the Holy of Holies would have been built, exactly at the foot of the northern scarp of es-Sakhra, which was originally cut for that purpose.

We now have three walls of the original Holy of Holies.

There was no wall on the eastern side of the Holy of Holies. It was separated from the main hall of the Temple (the Heichal, or Holy Place, as distinguished from the Holy of Holies) simply by a partition made of olive wood in Solomon's Temple and by a curtain or veil in Herod's Temple. Therefore, no signs of a partition would be visible on the sloping

---

*The steps cut into the western side of es-Sakhra, above the western scarp, appear to be the remains of a broad staircase that the Crusaders cut into the rock to lead up to their high altar.

surface east of es-Sakhra. Nevertheless, on the plan, we can easily plot the division line between the two chambers of the sanctuary. The curtain or veil was 20 cubits from the back wall.

It appears that on the east a gentle natural slope or ramp led up to the top of es-Sakhra, which, before the Crusaders' transformation of it, was much larger, with flat rock filling most of the Holy of Holies. The layers of rock in the ramp can be observed from the northern side of the balustrade as if the layers were in section, as they are in the balk of an archaeological excavation. Near the top of es-Sakhra, the thin rock layers of which the mountain is made up are horizontal; towards the east, however, they dip down to the level of the pavement near the eastern balustrade. It appears that the bedrock continues to slope down in an easterly direction below the pavement. I believe that this slope continues downwards until it reaches the general depth of 3 feet, 3 inches, below the floor.

While this indicates that the bedrock originally formed a ramp leading to the top of es-Sakhra,[13] the slope has been somewhat affected by Crusader quarrying. Many quarry marks on the sloping surface of the eastern part of es-Sakhra are still visible. It is generally agreed that this is the result of the Crusader practice of raising money by selling pieces of es-Sakhra for their weight in gold.

In the Temple of Solomon and in its later reconstructions, the eastern slope would have served as a ramp for the high priest to ascend once a year, on Yom Kippur, to the Holy of Holies.

The upper surface of es-Sakhra is difficult to see from ground level. It is easier to examine by means of photographs taken from high up, under the dome. On the northern side, the top is approximately 10 feet wide; it widens to about 20 feet in the south. The southern part is a little over 4 feet above the floor. The highest point, in the middle, is nearly 6 feet above the floor.

Two depressions are visible in the northern half. The southerly one is what looks to be an artificially cut trapezoid spreading out to the west. In the deepest part, no rock is visible, only small stones and mortar. It has been suggested that this place may be of special importance as the planting place of a tree for Asherah. However, as this depression is located at the very center of the Dome of the Rock, it may have played a role as the central pivot from which the plan of the Dome of the Rock was set out on the ground for its construction.

Just to the north of this trapezoidal depression is a rectangular depression that I believe is of extraordinary significance. My attention was first drawn to this feature on a flight to Israel in the spring of 1994. I remember the moment well—we were flying at 30,000 feet. Having averted my gaze from the in-flight video, I had taken out of my briefcase a large photograph of es-Sakhra.

Using the flat areas on the south of es-Sakhra as a starting point, I had already tentatively traced the walls of the Holy of Holies and needed merely to confirm this on-site. Then suddenly I noticed that in the middle of this square room was a dark rectangle! The first thing that came to mind was, of course, the former location of the Ark of the Covenant, which once stood in the center of the Holy of Holies in Solomon's Temple. But that surely could not be true, I thought. It must have been something else. Although very excited, I was determined not to be carried away. I needed to investigate this properly, treating es-Sakhra as one of the many archaeological sites I had worked on. I knew that if I were to claim such a function for the rectangular depression without proper investigation I would be dismissed as a sensationalist crank, as has happened to many others who have claimed to have found the Ark of the Covenant or to have identified its former location on the Temple Mount or elsewhere in the world.

I have tried to debunk this theory by thinking of other explanations for this rectangular depression in the center of the Holy of Holies. The only other possibility I have thought of is that it might be a column base for a statue. Early Christian pilgrims to the Temple Mount tell of seeing two statues on the site of the former Temple. Could this depression be the base for one of those statues? But column bases on which statues were erected are always square. This depression was rectangular; it measured 4 feet, 4 inches, by 2 feet, 7 inches. It was also far too small, according to Roman classical proportions, for a Roman column base of any height; and these statues, if they existed here at all (and the sources are not fully reliable), were designed to impress. Furthermore, the Roman temple to Jupiter, which was also mentioned in these sources, would have stood on the highest spot on the Temple Mount, using es-Sakhra as a podium, with the statues either to the west or east of it, not inside it. The result would have been that es-Sakhra was effectively buried and protected during this period.

According to Josephus, the Holy of Holies in Herod's Temple was completely empty: "In this stood nothing whatever: unapproachable, inviolable, invisible to all, it was called the Holy of Holy."[14] Josephus was apparently unaware of the existence of this most interesting feature.

According to my plan, this depression falls exactly in the center of the Holy of Holies. Converting its dimensions into cubits produces another rather startling fact. It measures exactly 1.5 by 2.5 cubits (2 feet, 7 inches, by 4 feet, 4 inches, or 80 centimeters by 130 centimeters). These are the dimensions of the Ark of the Covenant the Lord told Moses to build in the wilderness (Exodus 25:10), the ark that was ultimately placed in Solomon's Temple.

In the end, the conclusion that this unique depression marked the emplacement of the Ark of the Covenant inside the Holy of Holies is inescapable.

The Biblical text contains strong indications that a special "place" was prepared for the Ark of the Covenant within the Holy of Holies. In I Kings 8:6, we are told "The priests brought in the Ark of the Covenant of YHWH to *its place*, in the *dvir* [oracle, or speaking place] of the Temple" (italics added). Such a sacred object could not be left to wobble about on the uneven surface but would need a stable base on which to stand. The cutting of a flat basin such as this was the obvious solution.

In 1 Kings 8:20-21, Solomon declares that he has "built the Temple for the name of YHWH, God of Israel. And I have *set* there a place for the ark in which is the covenant of YHWH that he made with our fathers when he brought them out of the land of Egypt" (italics added). The Hebrew verb that is translated here as "set" (שם, seem) can also mean "put" or "make." In light of this depression on es-Sakhra, I would now translate this verse "I have *made* there a place for the ark."

One thing still mystified me about this depression—its orientation, with the short side facing the partition separating the Holy of Holies from the main hall of the Temple. Most depictions of this scene show the ark standing in the Tabernacle or in the Temple with its long side facing the partition. It is now clear that it stood with the short side facing the partition. A little thought reveals that this was the only way it could have stood. Otherwise, the priests would not have been able to take out the staves or poles by which it was carried. 1 Kings 8:8 explains that "the staves [also translated as "poles"] were so long that the ends of the staves were seen out in the Holy Place [the main hall of the sanctuary]." According to the Talmud (*Yoma* 54a), the staves were 10 cubits long. The Holy of Holies was only 20 cubits square. If the priests carrying the staves had turned the ark so that the long side faced the partition they would not have been able to remove the staves after placing the ark in the center of the Holy of Holies. The only way to remove the staves was by keeping the short side facing the partition that separated the Holy of Holies from the Holy Place.

When Herod rebuilt the Second Temple, he raised the entire structure by building it on a foundation 6 cubits high. Instead of a ramp leading up to es-Sakhra, the level of the Temple floor was reached by a 12-stepped staircase outside the Temple, in front of the porch, as described in *Middot* 3.6. The ramp was completely buried below the pavement of the new Temple floor. Only the very top of es-Sakhra remained visible inside the Holy of Holies. This new Temple floor was a little lower than the top of es-Sakhra, which was still the floor of the Holy of Holies. This explains a passage in the Mishnah (*Yoma* 5.2) describing the activities in the Temple on the Day of Atonement (Yom Kippur) in the Second Temple period, that is, "after the ark had been taken away": A stone in the otherwise empty Holy of Holies is referred to as the Foundation Stone (*Even ha-Shetiyah*), which "was higher than the ground by three fingerbreadths."

The Mishnah describes in some detail how on Yom Kippur the incense was ladled into a firepan by the high priest, how it was heaped upon the coals and how the firepan was placed on the Foundation Stone, the *Even ha-Shetiyah*: "On this [the Foundation Stone] he [the high priest] used [before the Roman destruction of the Temple] to put [the firepan]."

I believe that, when the Second Temple still stood, the high priest on Yom Kippur would place his censer or firepan in this depression—the same place where, during the First Temple period, the Ark of the Covenant stood.

ENDNOTES

CHAPTER 1

[1] According to the first century A.D. Jewish historian, Josephus, Herod began to build the Temple in the 18th year of his reign (19 B.C.); The Temple itself took only 18 months to build and the cloisters were completed within eight years. However, a reference in the Gospel of John (John 2:20—"It has taken 46 years to build this Temple"), suggests that the project continued for a much longer time.

[2] The original architect on this excavation was Munya Dunayevsky, who had collaborated closely with Professor Mazar on many earlier excavations for over 30 years until his untimely death in 1969. Dunayevsky made a major contribution to the initial stratigraphical analysis of the site, and his drawing of the southwest corner of the Temple Mount shows the preliminary understanding of the superstructure of the western wall.

Following Dunayevsky's death, the Irish architect Brian Lalor introduced the technique of three-dimensional reconstruction drawing to the dig. The basic concept of the reconstruction of the area around the Temple Mount is his. Lalor's catalogue of architectural elements provided an overview of the composite style employed in Herodian architecture. It was he who first suggested that Robinson's Arch supported, not a bridge, but a monumental stairway.

Following in Lalor's footsteps came David Sheehan, another Irish architect, and Leen Ritmeyer, from Holland. David Sheehan worked out some of the problems of the street adjacent to the western wall, adding the shops for which evidence had been found and the flight of steps that led up over them alongside the western wall. Details of Leen Ritmeyer's contribution are contained in this chapter.

CHAPTER 4

[1] R.A.S. Macalister, "The Rock-Cut Tombs in Wady er-Rababi, Jerusalem," *Palestine Exploration Fund Quarterly Statement* 1900-1901.

[2] Knut Olaf Dalman, "Uber ein Felsengrab im Hinnomtale bei Jerusalem," *Zeitschrift des deutschen Palästina-Vereins* 1939, Bd. 62, pp. 190-208.

CHAPTER 5

[1] Charles Wilson and Charles Warren, *Recovery of Jerusalem* (London: Bently, 1871), chap. 7, "Tanks and *Souterrains* of the Sanctuary," pp. 204-217.

[2] Jan Simons, *Jerusalem in the Old Testament* (Leiden: Brill, 1952), p. 355.

[3] Wilson and Warren, *Recovery of Jerusalem*, pp. 209-213.

[4] Warren, *Plans, Elevations, Sections, etc., showing the results of the Excavations at Jerusalem, 1867-1870, executed for Committee of the Palestine Exploration Fund* (PEF) (London: PEF, 1884), pls. VI, VII.

[5] *Biblical Archaeology Today*, Proceedings of the International Congress on Biblical Archaeology, Jerusalem, April 1984, ed. Janet Amitai (Jerusalem: Israel Exploration Society [IES], 1985), p. 484.

[6] Warren and Claude Condor, *Survey of Western Palestine, Jerusalem* (London: PEF, 1884), p. 215. See also, Warren, *Plans, Excavations, Sections, etc.*, pl. XII, secs. O-R.

[7] Strabo, *Geography* 16.40.

[8] This small valley was called St. Anne's Valley by Wilson, Chaphenatha Valley by Conrad Schick (*Die Stifshutte*, Tf. 4) and more recently the Beth Zetha Valley by Dan Bahat (*Carta's Historical Atlas of Jerusalem* [Jerusalem: Carta, 1983], p. 11).

[9] Josephus, *Antiquities of the Jews* 14.4.2.

[10] See Bahat, *Carta's Historical Atlas*, pp. 55, 61.

[11] Warren, *Plans, Elevations, Sections, etc.*, pls. II and VI.

[12] Josephus, *Antiquities of the Jews* 14.4.2.

[13] See George A. Smith, *Jerusalem, From the Earliest Times to A.D. 70* (London: Hodder and Stoughton, 1908), vol. 2, p. 588, n. 3: 20.67 inches = sacred cubit. See also Arye Ben David, "The Hebrew-Phoenician Cubit," *Palestine Exploration Quarterly* (PEQ) (1970), pp. 27-28: the Philaeterian-Ptolemaic cubit = 525 mm (20.67 inches). Joachim Jeremias (*Jerusalem in the Time of Jesus* [London: SCM, 1969], p. 11) defines the Philaeterian cubit as equal to 525 mm, or almost 21 inches. He quotes Didymus (end of first century A.D.) "who calculates the Egyptian cubit of Roman times as 1 1/2 Ptolemaic feet." As this foot was 350 mm long, the cubit was 1.5 X 350 = 525 mm. David Ussishkin, "The Original Length of the Siloam Tunnel," *Levant* 8 (1976), pp. 82-95: cubit = 52.5 cm (= 20.67 inches). Cf. Asher S. Kaufman, "Determining the Length of the Medium Cubit," *PEQ* 116 (1984), p. 131. Kaufman is close, but his measurement is not exact (20.319 inches instead of 20.66925). My own research has shown that 500 cubits of 20.67 inches equals exactly the distance from the step to the eastern wall, and therefore I believe that this was the cubit used for laying out the 500-cubit-square Temple Mount.

This cubit originated in Egypt and is also called the Egyptian long cubit; the short cubit was only 450 mm long. The long cubit is also known as the royal cubit, and had been in use since the 15th century B.C. This cubit later became known as the Philaeterian cubit, after the family name of the kings of Pergamum.

[14] Warren and Condor, *Survey of Western Palestine*, p. 146: "[T]he general direction of the east wall with south wall, as determined by the Survey, is 92 degrees 50 minutes. The eastern wall is somewhat irregular, the first 120 feet only being in a straight line; beyond this are several bulges, but it is probable that below the surface the first 260 feet of wall are in a straight line. At this point

there is a small postern on about the same level as the Single Gate on the south side. From this postern the wall takes a slight bend to north-east, so that at 650 feet from south-east angle it is about 8 feet to east of a line in production of first 260 feet." Simons also noted this bend to the northeast, and corrected its location to 240 feet from the southeast corner (*Jerusalem in the Old Testament*, p. 370) : "The first section of the [east] wall, from the same [S.E.] angle to a point 73.20 meters [= 240 feet] to the north, is practically straight but at this point it bends slightly outward, to the north-east, so that after 200 meters [= 650 feet] it is already 2.5 meters [= 8 feet] outside the line of the southern section."

[15] Josephus, *Antiquities of the Jews* 12.6.7.

[16] See Yoram Tsafrir, "The Location of the Seleucid Akra in Jerusalem," in *Jerusalem Revealed*, ed. Yigael Yadin (Jerusalem: IES, 1975), pp. 85-86. More recently, Gregory J. Wightman, "Temple Fortresses in Jerusalem, Part 1: The Ptolemaic and Seleucid Areas," *Bulletin of Anglo-Israel Archaeological Society* 9 (1989-1990), pp. 29-40.

[17] Josephus, *The Jewish War* 1.1.4.

[18] Josephus, *Antiquities of the Jews* 12.9.3.

[19] Tsafrir ("Location of the Seleucid Akra," pp. 85-86) accepts the southeastern hill of Jerusalem for the location of the Akra and correctly places it to the south of the Temple indeed close to our suggested location. We prefer, however, to place the Akra near the center of the southern Temple Mount wall, above cistern 11, from which it would have been easier to control the city and the southern access to the Temple Mount, and not near the southeast corner, as Tsafrir suggests. It would have been better to construct a fortress that could overlook the Temple Mount at the summit of the southeastern hill, rather than on the much lower slopes near the southeastern corner. Tsafrir's suggestion of identifying the masonry to the north of the "straight joint" in the eastern wall with the foundation of the Akra contradicts the statement of Josephus that the Akra was razed to the ground; it seems more logical to identify this stretch of Hellenistic masonry with the enlargement of the Temple Mount during the Hasmonean period.

[20] Josephus (*Antiquities of the Jews* 14.16.2) relates that when Herod, after he was made king, took Jerusalem and the Temple Mount, "the cloisters that were about the Temple were burnt."

[21] I would like to thank Dr. Rupert Chapman, secretary of the Palestine Exploration Fund, and Shimon Gibson, the photographic officer, for their help and cooperation in obtaining a copy of Simpson's painting of the "Great Sea."

[22] In his recently published book, *Mamluk Jerusalem*, Michael Burgoyne has identified a 4-meter-wide Herodian wall running east-west along the southern edge of the Antonia rock plateau. This wall, the southern wall of the Antonia fortress, is in line with the preserved northeast corner of the Temple Mount.

[23] Although the underground passageway originally leading to it from the inside was still used by the priests (see further, endnote 29).

[24] Father Pierre Benoit, O.P., "The Archaeological Reconstruction of the Antonia Fortress," in Yadin, *Jerusalem Revealed*, pp. 87-89.

[25] Warren, *Plans, Elevations, Sections, etc.*, pl. XXXII.

[26] Josephus, *The Jewish War* 5.51: "At first the plain at the top was hardly sufficient for the holy house and the altar, for the ground about it was very uneven, and like a precipice."

[27] The most famous of these is Asher Kaufman's. See his article "Where the Ancient Temple of Jerusalem Stood," **BAR**, March/April 1983. Kaufman places the Temple over a small monument known as the Dome of the Tablets, northwest of es-Sakhra. Kaufman's suggestion has been supported by Lawrence D. Sporty (*Biblical Archaeologist*, March 1991, pp. 28-35). Kaufman's theoretical location of the Temple over the Dome of the Tablets has several weaknesses: (1) He completely ignores the most important topographical data of the area north of the Muslim Platform—(A) the fosse, or moat observed by Warren, (B) the Bezetha Valley to the east of this moat and (C) the rock scarp under the northern edge of the Muslim Platform. The northern court of Kaufman's Temple would fall into the Bezetha Valley! Near the eastern wall, this valley is 160 feet lower than the es-Sakhra! (2) The floor under the Dome of the Tablets, where Kaufman located the Temple, is a stone—apparently a large paving slab or other stone in secondary use—and not

bedrock. Bedrock is at least 8 feet below the floor of this small monument. Thus, this location is by no means the top of the hill, as Josephus described the Temple's location. (3) Es-Sakhra, by contrast, is about 15 feet higher than Kaufman's location for the Temple. On this point alone, his theory is untenable. (4) His interpretations of the bedrock formations near the northwest corner of the Muslim Platform are highly dubious. Moreover, he failed to recognize the most important remains in this area: the step/wall, which is crucial in identifying and defining the square Temple Mount.

[28] For the other theories, see Melchior de Vogüé, *Le Temple de Jérusalem* (Paris, 1864); James Fergusson, *The Temples of the Jews and the other buildings in the Haram area at Jerusalem* (London, 1878); Charles Warren, *The Temple or the Tomb* (London, 1880); Claude R. Condor, "Statement of the Principal Controversies, II. Site of the Temple," *Survey of Western Palestine* (Jerusalem and London, 1884); Conrad Schick, *Die Stiftshütte, der Tempel in Jerusalem und der Tempelplatz der Jetztzeit* (Berlin, 1896); Charles M. Watson, *The site of the Temple* (London: PEF, 1896); Carl Mommert, *Topographie des alten Jerusalem, Zweiter Teil: Das Salomonische Tempel—und Palast—quartier auf Moriah* (Leipzig, 1903); Gustaf Dalman, "Der Zweite Tempel zu Jerusalem," *Palastina-Jahrbuch*, 5 (1909); F.J. Hollis, *The Archaeology of Herod's Temple* (London, 1934); Louis-H. Vincent, "Le Temple Hérodien d'après la Misnah," *Revue Biblique* 61 (1954); Asher S. Kaufman, "The meaning of Har Habayit and its northern gate," *Niv Hamidrashia* 18/19 (1984/1985); Benjamin Mazar, "The Temple Mount," *Biblical Archaeology Today* (Jerusalem: IES, 1985).

[29] Additional support for this location can be derived from the position of the underground cisterns, as surveyed by Warren. All of the cisterns, apart from cistern 12, fall outside the sanctuary, as I have located the Temple. (One would hardly expect to find people drawing water within the sanctuary itself.) As I have located the Temple, the large cistern 5 would be situated next to the Water Gate, which was near the altar, thus providing a convenient source of water for the service of the Temple.

With this location of the Temple, one can go on to identify a few more elements of the original Temple. *Middot* 1:3 describes the Tadi Gate as being "on the north, serving no purpose at all." It also mentions that if "one of [the priests] should have a nocturnal emission of semen, he goes out, proceeding along the passage that leads below the building—and lamps flicker on this side and that—until he reaches the immersion room. Rabbi Eliezer ben Jacob says, 'He goes out by the passage which leads below the rampart (*chel*), and so he came to the Tadi Gate.'"

Both Warren and Condor concluded that if cisterns 1 and 3 were extended farther to the north, they would meet exactly at a point in the rock scarp where they placed the Tadi Gate (*Survey of Western Palestine*, Jerusalem, p. 218). Cistern 1 was probably the passageway reached by descending from the Chamber of the Hearth, which was one of the three gates on the north of the inner court of the Temple, while cistern 3 was the immersion room itself. *Middot* continues, that there were "four offices in the Chamber of the Hearth; ... [T]hrough that on the northwestern side do they go down to the room for immersion" (*Middot* 1:5). Despite the fact that the Tadi Gate was put out of use by Herod's northern extension, the underground passage was still used by the priests to visit the immersion room (see endnote 23).

It is also interesting to note that this passageway (cistern 1) is exactly in line with the rock under the Dome of the Rock, and also with the passageways of the Double Gate. Using either the northern Tadi Gate or the southern Hulda Gates, the pilgrim of the past would always see first whatever was built over that rock, whether altar, porch, the Holy or most probably the Holy of Holies of the Temple. The importance of this architectural alignment shows that these gates were built according to a uniform plan.

This southern route passes in between cisterns 6 and 36, which according to Ronnie Reich might have been *mikva'ot* ("Two Possible Miqva'ot on the Temple Mount," *Israel Exploration Journal* 39 [1989], pp. 63-65). Reich suggests, however, that these *mikva'ot* were located outside the early Temple Mount.

CHAPTER 6

[1] Ephraim Stern, ed., *The New Encyclopedia of Archaeological Excavations in the Holy Land* (New York: Simon & Schuster, 1993), vol. 2, p. 718.

[2]Josephus, *The Jewish War* 5.184, and *Antiquities of the Jews* 15.398.

[3]Charles Clermont-Ganneau, *Archaeological Researches in Palestine During the Years 1873-1874* (London: Palestine Exploration Fund, 1899), vol. 1, pp. 216-217.

[4]I would like to thank Joseph G. Hurley, Esq., and his wife Davia Solomon, Esq., for their continued support in the form of a second generous grant through the Biblical Archaeology Society for this work. A travel grant from the Rothschild Foundation made it possible for my family and me to spend considerable time in Jerusalem during the spring and summer of 1994 while I did the post-doctoral research on which this chapter is based, under the supervision of Professor Gideon Foerster of the Hebrew University.

[5] Gustaf Dalman, "Der heilige Felsen von Jerusalem," *Neue Petra-Forschungen und der heilige Felsen von Jerusalem* (Leipzig: J.C. Hinrich, 1912). See also Hans Schmidt, *Der heilige Fels in Jerusalem* (Tübingen: J.C.B. Mohr, 1933).

[6]Josephus, *Antiquities* 15.391.

[7]Fulcher of Chartres, *A History of the Expedition to Jerusalem, 1095-1127*, trans. F.R. Ryan (Knoxville: Univ. of Tennessee Press; 1969), pp. xxxi, 1, 5-10.

[8]F. Gabrieli, *Arab Historians of the Crusades* (Berkeley and Los Angeles: Univ. of California Press, 1969), pp. 168-171.

[9]Gabrieli, *Arab Historians*, p. 171.

[10]Guy Le Strange, *Palestine under the Moslems* (Beirut: Khayats, 1890; reprint 1965), p. 132.

[11]Dalman, *Neue Petra-Forschungen*, p. 125.

[12]Retired Hebrew University physics professor Asher Kaufman shows two different orientations for the First and Second temples, although there is no historical proof that this was so.

His orientation of the Second Temple is based on the assumption that the Temple was trapezoidal in shape. As evidence, he relies on a glass fragment of the Byzantine period that shows a painting of the Temple with surrounding walls. These walls are drawn in perspective, a normal artistic procedure, and the resulting tapering shape cannot therefore be used as archaeological evidence that the Temple was trapezoidal. He then tries to match this idea up with some very small bedrock cuts and the directions of water cisterns to prove his point.

His orientation of the First Temple is derived from another small bedrock cut to the north of the platform of the Dome of the Rock (see **BAR**, March/April 1983, picture on p. 48 and text on p. 56). It is true that these bedrock cuts were probably part of the foundation trenches of a building, but they are insufficient in themselves to prove that they were part of the Temple. (I believe that they may have had something to do with the foundations of the Towers of Hananeel and Mea, which were later replaced by the Baris.) He also claims that his "Find 14" was a "crypt supporting the northeastern angle of the Court of Priests and part of the Outer Court" (p. 56). Warren, who discovered this vault in Cistern 29, wrote, "The vault itself seems clearly to be Arab work not earlier than the 13th century" (with Claude R. Conder, *The Survey of Western Palestine, Jerusalem* [London: Palestine Exploration Fund, 1884], p. 224). To incorporate a medieval structure into the First Temple is archaeologically impossible, to say the least.

Kaufman's interpretation of these remains hinges, of course, on a partially broken paving slab below the so-called Dome of the Spirits, which he claims was the Foundation Stone. However, the shape of this stone, with a rectangular projection on its eastern side, makes it abundantly clear that it is indeed a paving slab. The purpose of this rectangular projection is to enable a smaller paving slab to be laid next to it. Kaufman's theory also contradicts Josephus's historical record that the Temple stood on the summit of the mountain. The bedrock below Kaufman's paving slab, which, incidentally, is smaller than other paving slabs found in front of the Double and Triple Gates, is about 16 feet lower than es-Sakhra according to Warren's plans! The slab is also far too small for a foundation of the Temple, as the Holy of Holies alone was about ten times larger than this stone.

Additionally, it is archaeologically unsound to use the orientation of cisterns to prove the orientation of a building above. Cisterns are usually round or cut at right angles to the bedrock formation, which is not necessarily the direction of the building above.

The opinion of the archaeological community as to Kaufman's theory is summed up in Stern, *New Encyclopedia*, vol. 2, p. 743: "An attempt by A. Kaufman to 'shift' the location of the Temple slightly to the north of this traditional site [of the Dome of the Rock], relying on unclear archaeological remains he ascribes to the Second Temple period and on other evidence, lacks concrete proof."

[13]This is confirmed by Clermont-Ganneau's other observations in the northern part of the Dome of the Rock, where he found bedrock, in general, a meter below the floor of the Dome of the Rock. In 1959 Bellarmino Bagatti (*Recherches sur le site du Temple de Jérusalem (Ier-VIIe siecle)* [Jerusalem: Franciscan Printing Press, 1979], pp. 28-29) noticed bedrock at several places below the floor during repair operations conducted at that time.

[14]Josephus, *Jewish War* 5.219.

RITMEYER ARCHAEOLOGICAL DESIGN

Exciting educational materials for lovers of Israel and Biblical Archaeology
(prices include shipping by airmail):

THE TEMPLE AND THE ROCK. This 60-page study
booklet, written in 1996, documents each stage of the
research into the ancient Temple Mount. A total of 32
illustrations, most of which are published here for the
first time, explain and clarify the text. *$20.00.*

The Temple and the Rock

SLIDE SETS (36 SLIDES):
• ALEC GARRARD'S MODEL OF THE 2ND TEMPLE.
Explore the world of the Second Temple in this slide set
of Alec Garrard's beautiful Temple model. *$47.00,
including caption booklet.*

• JERUSALEM IN 30 A.D.
Artistic reconstruction drawings and on-site photographs transport you back 2,000
years to first-century A.D. Jerusalem. *$47.00, including caption booklet.*

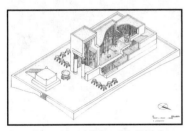

Reconstruction of Solomon's Temple

• FROM SINAI TO SAKHRA.
Follow the Ark of the Covenant from its
construction by Bezaleel in the Sinai Desert
to its installation in the Holy of Holies of
Solomon's Temple in Jerusalem. *$47.00,
including caption booklet.*

SLIDE SETS (60 SLIDES):
• THE ARCHAEOLOGY OF HEROD'S TEMPLE MOUNT.
Views of the recent excavations, a newly designed
architectural model and detailed reconstruction
drawings recreate the splendour of the first-century
A.D. Temple. *$82.50, including caption booklet.*

• WORSHIP AND RITUAL IN HEROD'S TEMPLE.
This latest slide set has been designed to convey an idea
of the ritual of the Temple in the time of Christ. The set
includes views of the most recent model of the Temple,
artifacts and appropriate photographs of the natural
world. *$82.50, including caption booklet.*

#7. The Golden Vine of the Temple

BLACK-AND-WHITE POSTERS:
- Reconstruction of the Temple Mount in Jerusalem
- The development of the Temple Mount during the Second Temple period
- Reconstruction of the settlement of Qumran
- Reconstruction of the northern palaces of Masada

Each approx. 25"-wide poster costs $7.50 + $5.00 airmail for up to 2 posters.
Hand-colored versions of these posters are available upon request
for $25.00 + $5.00 airmail each.

COLOR POSTERS:
- The facade of the Temple with the Court of the Women from Alec Garrard's model of Herod's Temple
- Jerusalem in 30 A.D. with explanatory leaflet detailing a route around the city in the time of Christ

Each approx. 25"-wide poster costs $15.00 + $5.00 airmail for up to 2 posters.

CIBACHROME (NON-FADE) PRESENTATION PHOTOGRAPHS:
1. Herod's Temple from the southeast
2. Herod's Temple and the Court of the Women from the east
3. View of the Eastern Gate, the Court of the Women and the Court of the Priests
4. Inside the Court of the Women showing Levites singing on the 15 semicircular steps
5. The facade of Herod's Temple
6. The Court of the Priests with the Altar and Laver
7. The Golden Vine of Herod's Temple

$35.00 each. Special offer: Buy all seven cibachromes for the price of six ($210.00).

#4. Inside the Court of the Women

MODEL OF HEROD'S TEMPLE MOUNT:
The historical sources and the excavations around the Temple Mount that followed the Six-Day War formed the basis for the design of this magnificent model of Jerusalem's Temple Mount. Hand-cast in high-quality resin, it measures 11.5"x7"x1.75", a convenient size for study by small groups around a table. *$410.00.*